THE
MOUNTAIN BIKE
SKILLS MANUAL
FITNESS & SKILLS FOR EVERY RIDER

CLIVE FORTH

A&C Black • London

◎ NOTE

Whilst every effort has been made to ensure that the content of this book is as technically accurate and as sound as possible, neither the author nor the publishers can accept responsibility for any injury or loss sustained as a result of the use of this material.

Published by A&C Black Publishers Ltd
36 Soho Square, London W1D 3QY
www.acblack.com

ISBN 978 1 4081 2732 2

A CIP catalogue record for this book is available from the British Library.

Acknowledgements
Cover photograph © Frazer Waller
Inside photographs © Frazer Waller
Designed by Steve Russell
Commissioned by Charlotte Croft
Edited by Kate Turvey

This book is produced using paper that is made from wood grown in managed, sustainable forests. It is natural, renewable and recyclable. The logging and manufacturing processes conform to the environmental regulations of the country of origin.

Typeset in 9pt Helvetica Neue on 11pt leading by Saxon Graphics Ltd, Derby

Printed and bound in China by South China Printing Co

CONTENTS_

Acknowledgements iv

Foreword v

Introduction 1

1 A BRIEF HISTORY 3

2 THE BIKES 11

3 RECREATIONAL RIDING 33

4 COMPETITION 55

5 EQUIPMENT 89

6 SKILLS AND TECHNIQUE 109

Glossary 196

Further reading and useful websites 200

Index... 201

ACKNOWLEDGEMENTS_

I would like to thank my parents for believing in me and supporting me for all those years, R.I.P.

I would also like to thank the following:

Charlotte Croft and the staff at A&C Black for giving me the opportunity to share my knowledge with you. Frazer Waller for all the laughs and for the sweet photos.

Rob Lee for his words and for the many experiences we have shared growing up together. Ian Warby for the foreword and friendship – this book might never have been written if Ian and I hadn't met. Beeg, Jockey, Fev, Gavin, Phil, Jan, Guy, Steve, Matt M, Bart, Dan Dare and all the old-school locals. Adam Jakeman and John Flood, who we so dearly miss, R.I.P.

Titley, Collins boy, Beard, Steve, Will, Rory, Tim and all the riders from back in the day. Tally, Wendy, Jamie, Robbie, Craig, Jemma, Andy, Elayna, Andy H and all the locals of Mabie Forest. Big Dave and Dr Ju for looking after me and keeping my body in check. My sponsors Syncros Endurance, Santa Cruz, Dakine, Exposure, Osprey, Neo Guard and Skins.

Scotby cycles – www.bikebike.co.uk

The Shed, Mabie Forest – thank you for my second home/office.

i-Cycles, Innerleithen.

Rik and Drumlanrig Cycle Museum. The folks at Bike Park Fenasosa in Spain for their hospitality – www.lafenasosa.com. 7stanes and Forestry Commission Scotland. Rich and Craig from Cycle-Wise. Chaineys Cycles. Roy Pink Cycles. Phil Corley.

And finally, the early pioneers and anyone who loves riding off road.

Clive Forth
MTBSkills – www.mtbskills.eu

FOREWORD_

Mountain biking was still very much in its infancy when Clive and I first met as teenagers in the early nineties. We both lined up on many a windswept start line, ready to take on a freshly cut trail through a wood or a forest or just around a farmer's field. Mountain bike racing was an overnight success but, today, it's about far more than racing – it's the freedom that comes from riding a mountain bike out on the trail, at one with nature and the bike.

If we fast forward 20 years from those early races, Clive's book illustrates how mountain biking has grown and flourished into a global phenomenon. History is something we often take for granted, so why look back when there's so much more to look forward to? After all, isn't one of the mainstays in our skills instruction: 'Look for the nearest high point to you as far down the trail as you can see it'?

For mountain bikers, our history and our roots are important (we're not talking visual performance cues here). Mountain bikers have shaped the way we ride, where we ride and what we ride. In life, people talk about a person's fingerprint being seen across their chosen field and Clive's is undoubtedly across mountain biking. As a close friend and confidant, I've witnessed Clive's influence – his insight and skills as a rider have enabled him to spot new trends in mountain biking and take the lead in many new mountain bike disciplines and locations, way before they break through to the mainstream.

Clive's father, Bob, was a talented amateur racing car driver; he ensured that Clive had a good understanding of the physics of speed from an early age. This, along with Clive's natural flair and ability to 'manage energy', makes him a natural on a mountain bike. Riding with Clive, and witnessing his skills first hand, heavily influenced the development of my mountain bike skills training system, right from the very early days of its inception and development. His skills and ability as a downhiller, dual rider and dirt jumper back in the day certainly made me ask questions in my mind; the answers have set the direction that the development of the skills system has taken me. You'll read all about Clive's insight into the world of skills coaching as you work your way through the book.

It's been said before, but as a rider Clive's been there, done it, got the t-shirt and cleaned his bike with it. His unique orbit and take on mountain biking gives him a great perspective. He shares that perspective in this book to take a look back at all the advances in mountain bike technology, trails and skills training, along with all the highs (and some lows) that have influenced and shaped mountain biking and a generation of mountain bikers, and continue to so. Read on and enjoy.

Ian Warby
Senior Development Officer for mountain biking at the Cyclists' Touring Club (CTC) and proprietor of Fire Crest Mountain Biking.

INTRODUCTION_

For me, riding is everything – it makes me who I am. I have ridden a bike for as long as I can remember and started racing way back in 1988. I used to race 100cc karts nationally but I was always frustrated at how inaccessible the sport was, whereas mountain biking was available 24/7. While I was growing up near multiple riding spots, the temptation of leaving my urban surroundings and escaping to the woods was overpowering. My friends and I would spend hours and hours at the local jump spots, messing around riding hills and getting air. We had a ball growing up and the playtime gave us a skill base that we often took for granted.

As the sport continued to grow in popularity, and more and more people began adopting the mountain bike and hitting trails, there arose an obvious need for guides and tutors. The one thing I noticed about the new breed of rider was their lack of technical ability and general knowledge of the sport. I could only put it down to the fact that they were in too much of a hurry to ride their bikes after a hectic week at work: they neglected to practise their core skills.

There was hardly anyone teaching the basic skills and I needed a new challenge: my company MTBSkills was formed. I set about breaking mountain biking down into a structured skills set and created various methods of delivering the message. I tried and tested my own theories over many years, both on the race course and on the trail, working with top racers, including the 2005 solo 24-hour World Champion Rob Lee. All of this was done before delivering sessions to the general public, and I have had nothing but positive feedback and top results with my work. When the opportunity came to put it all into print, I jumped at the chance.

The concept of the book is simple: read at your leisure and discover how the sport came to be, or simply dip in and out of the chapters to pick up hints and tips on how to improve your setup and riding skills. All the core skills have been captured in sequences to help you see the detail in body position and technique, and accompanying the photographs there is descriptive text to help you further your understanding. I have had great pleasure in producing this book and I hope you enjoy reading it. If you would like to further improve your riding ability, tutors at MTBSkills are available for skills sessions throughout the year.

A BRIEF HISTORY_

So where and when did mountain biking begin? As far as recorded history shows, the first bike ridden off road was coincidentally the first ever pedal cycle made. Kirkpatrick Macmillan, a blacksmith from Drumlanrig Castle in southern Scotland, built the first ever pedal cycle and rode it some 68 miles to Glasgow over mountainous terrain back in 1842. The bike was crude, cumbersome and lacked a critical component which, rumour has it, led to the first recorded road traffic accident in the British Isles. Fatigued from his epic ride, poor Kirkpatrick lost control of his bicycle on the slippery, cobbled streets of Glasgow and unfortunately injured a small child in the process.

There are rumours in modern Scottish mountain biking that Kirkpatrick consequently returned to Drumlanrig and invented the disc brake! As to how much truth there is to this I will leave to your own imagination. Throughout history, people have ridden bikes off road. The Italian army used bicycles in the First World War, and the legendary Annie Londonderry rode a bicycle around the world, starting her journey in 1897 and completing it fifteen months later in 1899, a truly epic off-road adventure which took her across Europe, Egypt, Singapore and back to the US.

A replica of the Kirkpatrick Macmillan bike can be seen at the bicycle museum at Drumlanrig Castle.

Raleigh produced the Bomber in the early 80s – a favoured bike of many kids in the UK.

What we do know from the available evidence is that, from 1955 onwards, a group of friends in the UK, known as the 'Rough Stuff Fellowship', modified bikes to ride off road on byways and dirt lanes. There is also evidence to show that the members made modifications to various existing production bicycles that included the addition of gears and cantilever brakes. Furthermore, custom frames were produced but in no huge quantities. I have also heard tales from some of my father's friends, brothers David and Ginger Marshall, a couple of guys who build championship-winning racing cars. They were putting front forks from mopeds on modified bikes and riding them in my old haunt Wendover Woods at a similar time.

There is also evidence out there that another guy from the UK, Geoff Apps, was designing frames and modifying existing bikes. His first custom creation was named the Range Rider, an off-road bike that incorporated a modified frame, built up with components from overseas. These bikes had knobby tyres, gears and the option of drum brakes or rim brakes. They were only built to order and it wasn't until the late seventies that small production runs started, which lasted for around 10 years. By this time, the US – whose off-road bike development had been running in parallel to European development – were starting to dominate the new scene of mountain biking. Their thirst for off-road fun, combined with the Eastern world producing affordable components in large quantities, essentially led to the creation of the modern mountain bike.

>> THE MARIN COUNTY MOVEMENT

History shows the key moment that led to the mass production of mountain bikes and the phenomenon that has grown to epic proportions today.

A group of friends in Marin County, California, known as the 'Larkspur Canyon Gang', started to ride and create trails on Mount Tamalpais in the late sixties. They lived at the bottom of the mountain and would ride old post-war paperboy bikes – given the name 'klunkers', and also known as cruisers, beaters, bombers or ballooners – up and around Mount Tam, as it was affectionately known. They made basic modifications to the bikes – things like the mud guards, chain guards and kick stands would be removed. The lack of gears meant that they would push the bikes up the mountain and mess around all day riding trails. They even had a few timed competitions for fun to see who was the fastest, just for a laugh: kids' stuff that inspired me to do similar things when I was growing up in the eighties.

Marc Vendetti from the Larkspur Canyon Gang joined a renegade group of road cyclists who created the outfit Velo Club Tamalpais in 1972.

Marc used to ride his klunker to club meetings at the Robson Harrington Mansion in San Francisco. The other members of Velo Club Tam showed an interest in his bike and were soon sourcing similar post-war bikes to modify. This key year was, for me, the point in time that man's sense of adventure and obsession with mechanical engineering fused together and exploded. A primeval testosterone-fuelled urge to push the envelope of mind, body and machine began.

Enter the racers and counter-culture roommates from 32 Humboldt Avenue in San Francisco. Great road racers Gary Fisher, Charlie Kelly, Joe Breeze and Alan Bonds were all members of Velo Club Tam. These guys got into the social klunker scene with friends Fred Wolf and Wende Cragg, to name but two. The vibrant music scene of that era influenced our early pioneers and I often relate my love of music to my riding and the rhythm of breathing. Finding a 'flow' in a trail can often be compared to musical composition.

There were obviously other people across the globe creating and enjoying their own scene in their own way, but something special would grow out of Marin County in the US. Although the Canyon Gang had a race in 1971, and another bunch of hippy dirt bike riders, the Morrow Dirt Club, were spotted by members of Velo Club Tam at a cyclo-cross race in 1974, it was the racers from Velo Club Tam who started to really push the boundaries. Inspired by the modifications the Morrow guys had made to their bikes, the larger group of friends from the San Francisco Bay area started to source components from local bike shops to upgrade and improve their klunkers.

>> THE ARMS RACE BEGINS

Where you have racers you inevitably have a competitive vibe, and the roommates of Marin County's new counter-culture pastime soon found themselves bantering about who was the fastest. Everyone was in agreement that the fun bit was the blast back down from the mountain after an all-day 'klunk', and that the flowing trails tested everyone's skills, while the rudimentary technology tested their nerves.

Enter Repack, a treacherous access track that runs up Mount Tam. This trail was used to host a series of downhill time trials in late 1976. Repack descends a terrifying 1,400 feet in just over two miles. The limited stopping power of the rear hub brake meant that riders had to learn to drift the bike sideways in order to slow down through turns rather than into them. This lack of stopping power often led to some skin loss and it was not long until front brakes were added to the old bikes.

This early Schwinn was converted into a trophy.

Huge brake levers provided slightly more stopping power than standard ones.

Limited technology also gave Repack its name – the never-ending job of repacking your coaster brake with grease because it had evaporated from the heat created on each run. Repack was one of the influential components for my own counter-culture experience of goofing around in the woods and tinkering with machines. Without a doubt, Repack started the arms race and the need for technological advantage. Forks were breaking, brakes were failing and the guys became masters at modifying the now-favoured Schwinn Excelsior X frame. But this 1940s hulk of steel was soon superseded by the first production run of custom-built mountain bikes in the US.

Joe Breeze worked with his father in San Francisco fabricating road bike frames and, when his friend Charlie Kelly asked him about the possibility of making a mountain bike frame, Joe hit the drawing board. Three months later Joe rode the new Breezer bike, as it rapidly became known, to first place in the Repack. At the same time Craig Mitche, an eccentric character known for producing alternative bicycles and recumbants, also fabricated and equipped a specific mountain bike frame. It actually looked quite conventional and similar to a modern cross-country mountain bike, as did the early bikes from the UK.

Joe's bikes were beautiful. They came equipped with specific components sourced from far and wide, finished with the essential pump, water-bottle cage, spare inner tube, patch kit and tyre levers – all the necessary items to help keep you rolling while out in the wilderness. The global off-road riding experience was growing but the US would lead the way in years to come.

These early mountain bikes had a wider spread of gear ratios compared to road bikes, as the riders soon discovered that the best way up and out to remote locations was by pedal power, something that Gary and the guys had plenty of. The 'Breezer' soon got the attention of everyone in the Bay Area and it was Gary Fisher's sharp eye that could see the demand and a new market.

Gary, Charlie and Alan had already started to source components and put together bikes for friends, as did many people on the scene. Then one day Gary was introduced to Tom Ritchey, who was a fantastic road racer and frame builder. Tom built the first run of bikes for Gary that would become the start of Fisher Mountain Bikes. There was another man on the scene at this time too – Mike Sinyard, a friend of Gary's. Mike rode some of the Fisher-Ritchey bikes and was very impressed. He could also see the popularity of riding off road for leisure growing on a global scale and went on to create Specialized Mountain Bikes. The first specific mountain bike was released by Specialized in 1981, backed up by a huge advertising campaign. By this time the globe was going crazy for the mountain bike.

As the bomb went off and quality bikes were available off the peg, it wasn't long until shiny magazines were gracing the shelves of newsstands in the UK. Cue me, aged 11, staring into the pages of *Mountain Bike Action*, entranced. Like most children I had to wait ('patience is a virtue', as my parents told me), and it was about 18 months after that first contact that I got a real mountain bike. Was this going to be another boom–bust fad that swept the world, or a global fever that would have riders fighting it out for Olympic Gold? I didn't care – the awe-inspiring pictures of people riding in the wilderness in California had me hooked. I would dream about escaping to the hills and sliding my bike on dirt.

>> THE EIGHTIES MOVEMENT

As the eighties moved on, the industry grew in strength, new companies were formed and the Far East rapidly became geared up to produce huge quantities of components over a wide variety of specifications. The US were manufacturing the exotic and desirable; the UK also had a hand in the global development, with established frame builders Chas Roberts and Dave Lloyd producing custom-built mountain bike frames, using components sourced from afar. Gears from Japan, brakes from Europe – it seemed everyone was at it.

The mid-eighties soon rolled around and the arrival of Far East imports in the UK really jump-started things. The availability of advanced technology in abundance opened the floodgates to a wider market, and clever distributors and bike shop owners were buying into the hype created predominately in the US.

Competitions were also appearing here in the UK and on the Continent. Clubs were popping up everywhere – federations like the National Off-Road Bicycle Association (NORBA) and the British Mountain Bike Federation (BMBF), among others, were formed and the scene flourished. Yet again the US led the way by creating a national series of competitions and heroes were being born on both sides of the Atlantic as the UK and Europe followed suit. Riders like Greg Herbold, Ned Overend and John Tomac were on posters in kids' bedrooms across the land. Some of the inspired kids of the eighties would later find themselves on posters, riding bikes and inspiring others to follow in their footsteps.

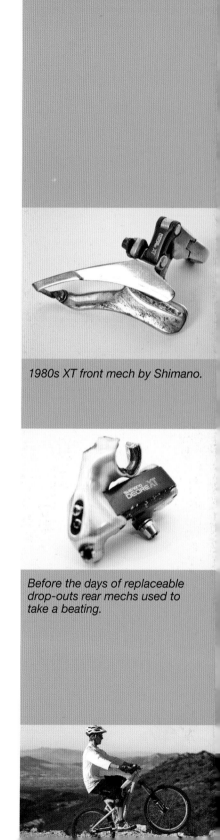

1980s XT front mech by Shimano.

Before the days of replaceable drop-outs rear mechs used to take a beating.

The Muddy Fox Courier.

Rory Hitchens still competes today and he also works in the industry developing new lighting systems.

>> THE NEXT PHASE

At this stage in the game, riders would have to compete in various disciplines to become National Champion. They had to be proficient in cross-country, downhill, uphill and trials to be crowned the best mountain biker. By 1990 the Union Cycliste Internationale (UCI), the world's governing body for cycling, sanctioned the first ever World Mountain Bike Championships in Durango, Colorado. However, the first unofficial (non UCI sanctioned) world championships took place a year earlier on Mammoth Mountain in California: Don Myrah won the men's cross country and Sarah Ballentyne took the women's. Hans Ray took top honours in the trials, John Tomac won the downhill and Britain's Tim Gould won the uphill. In the women's hill climb, Susan DeMattei took top honours and the dual slalom was won by Dave Cullinan of the US.

As the nineties progressed so did the riders and bikes. Just like the early pioneers, people were pushing the envelope, jumping bigger and riding further. The clothes, like the music of that era, were loud, and mountain biking was entering the mainstream in a big way. Corporate sponsors were backing riders and competitions – even new brands like Red Bull were gaining youth cult status through partnering with one of the fastest growing extreme sports in the world. Here in the UK, top men's magazine *GQ* even sponsored a race team to compete in the UCI World Cup Series. Similar progress was being made all through the developed world. With large partners on board, the new sport of mountain biking was looking to be more than a passing fad.

Competition was hotter than ever and we were starting to see the sport segregate into the different disciplines and genres you see today. Riders at the top level no longer had to compete in all the disciplines but could become masters and champions in a discipline of their choice. The UCI started to host a yearly world championship in downhill, cross-country, dual slalom and trials – an annual world cup series soon followed. Many nations were running sanctioned events in accordance with the UCI's rule book, creating national and international champions in the process.

The UK has always featured at the front of the field in all disciplines. Cross-country racer Tim Gould took Gold at the World Championships in the uphill at Mammoth and long-time friends Tim Flooks and Rory Hitchins also delivered a slice of the UK scene on foreign shores in the early 1990s. Another Brit, David Hemming, took a medal at the 1992 Worlds in Bromont, finishing second in the downhill, riding a full rigid Klein Attitude bike. Then there was the late Jason McRoy, an inspiration to many British mountain bikers. Jason was the first UK rider to sign with a major global brand and featured on the podium at the famous Kamikaze

downhill time trial on Mammoth Mountain in the US. A true legend in mountain bike history.

As the scene gathered momentum, there was also a need for new events to test the best. The renegade counter-culture approach of our early pioneers was in full effect in the mid-nineties, when the French outfit UCC (Union Confédérale de Coordination), directed by George Edwards, started organising marathon downhill events in the French Alps – yet another discipline that would inspire people to specialise in a particular field of this fantastic sport. They were not alone in their counter-culture approach, as the UCI failed to recognise the fast-growing scene of endurance cross country. In the US, 24-hour races started to take place and have grown in popularity to become one of the most popular forms of racing today.

>> THE PRESENT DAY

The sport seems to have kept up the pace, making mountain biking a hugely popular pastime and professional sport, backed by a multi-million dollar industry. Who knows where it will end up in the years to come? Riders will continue to push boundaries and manufacturers will inevitably develop products to keep up with their demands. To be honest, we have never had it so good, and it just keeps on getting better and better.

Mass start downhill racing.

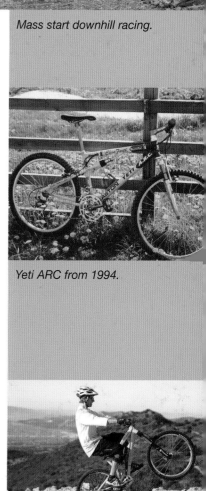

Yeti ARC from 1994.

THE BIKES_

By the late nineties, bikes were moving into a new phase, with hydraulic suspension, front forks and specific tyres for various terrains. Specialist clothing was filling the racks in bike shops across the world. Bikes were looking more like spaceships, disc brakes had followed on from hydraulic rim brakes, and rear suspension was everywhere.

The bike geometry had also changed several times as manufacturers established a multitude of standards for frames and components alike: bikes typically had 135mm rear axles, 110mm front axles, 1⅛-inch steerer tubes and headsets. Wheels were lighter and stronger and things were moving at a rapid rate. People would experiment with disc wheels, carbon fibre and metal alloy composites. I even saw a white tyre, produced by the company IRC, on a Japanese rider's bike in 1994, made from a super-soft compound rubber. A multitude of manufacturers progressed technology at such a rate, to a point where things inevitably started to slow down by the turn of the century.

That's not to say things are not still progressing – it's human nature that got us this far and that's something which is not going to change in a hurry. Rider input has polished all the component parts used in a mountain bike to such a high degree that the measurement in the improvement has narrowed significantly. However, as with all things, something comes along once in a while and stirs things up.

>> POST-SEVENTIES DEVELOPMENT

As we have discovered in the opening chapter, early bikes ridden in the mountains were just that – bikes. Today's mountain bikes are a long way away from the late sixties Schwinns but how did they become so? Early bike builders had no reference point when constructing frames. Sure, they knew they had to be stronger and lighter than the old klunkers but, when it came to geometry and its effect on the handling, they only had limited data to look at. Those early production bikes from the seventies and eighties were typically based on road bike geometry but had long top tubes with slacker angles than their road bike cousins. They came equipped with specific components that included cantilever or U brakes,

*Square taper Bottom Bracket
from the 80s.*

and over-bar seven-speed shifters, some of which were indexed (gears with a solid feel and an audible 'click' to them, rather than the previous gear shifters). The bike builders were using the industry standard one-inch steerer tube on the forks and the stem would drop down into this tube, with a quill holding it in place (the tubular section of the stem that inserts into the fork steerer tube is cut at 45 degrees like the end of a quill, hence the name).

We had to suffer the cup-and-cone setup in hubs, bottom brackets and headsets for some years before manufacturers started to use the now-favoured sealed cartridge bearings. Previous to this development, the rudimentary technology left riders rebuilding these key moving components more often than was desired. Loose ball bearings would have to be replaced and fresh grease applied accordingly, and the seals were poor so water damage was frequent.

Stopping power was limited, but cantilever and U brakes were definitely an upgrade on the old coaster brake and boot-to-floor method used by the early pioneers. One huge problem that rim brakes presented riders with (other than the lack of power in wet conditions) was the inconsistent nature of them. Having inevitably dented and buckled your soft aluminium rims, the brakes had a tendency to snatch or fade as the rim snaked pass them. Soft rims meant you had to make sure your brake pads were not touching your tyres, and this was a day-to-day chore. Hardcore enthusiasts would clean the pads and the rim often to avoid the grinding noise of brake pad on rim, and this also helped to improve the brakes' efficiency.

The ball bearings in cages seemed to disintegrate if they came within 100m of water.

Early cantilever designs looked cumbersome and were quite crude, but this would change as the years rolled on: by the late eighties, slimline versions with a slightly more rounded feel were seen on some bikes. Brake-lever design also had a rudimentary feel and look to it, showing little evidence of imagination, but soon bikes were equipped with levers

Here you can see the progression of the cantilever.

The V brake of the 1990s.

that matched the design aesthetic and finish of the cantilevers. These improved units had cams engineered into them, creating a more powerful, efficient brake. This soon became a common sales point for all major manufacturers.

To add to our woes, we had toe clips to help get some grip on the flat bear-trap style pedals. Shoes specifically designed for riding were just starting to appear in the late eighties. Up until then, people used to ride in skateboard shoes, walking boots and basic bike boots that resembled lightweight walking boots. Toe clips, as cumbersome as they are, definitely helped a whole load with both efficiency going uphill and grip while descending. Manufacturers produced a variety of pedals with slimline bodies and tabs for flicking the pedal round to help you get in the cage. They unfortunately spun on the aforementioned cup-and-cone bearing system.

By the late eighties, upgrade equipment was everywhere and retailers were stocking up on a vast array of new components and accessories for the riders and bikes. Polystyrene lightweight helmets offered more protection than previous options and, for those that could afford it, or in my case fit into it, Lycra was adopted from road cycling. The colours were bright and loud and had a skateboarder/surfer look to them – perhaps another spin-off from our hippie pioneers. Bikes sported neon and speckled paint jobs, and buzz brands like Marin, Kona and Muddy Fox were the talk in the playground for young enthusiasts.

Bike designs were becoming more radical, and frame builders produced specific trials mountain bikes for competition use. These bikes had 20-inch wheels with wide, sticky tyres and looked like long, low BMX bikes, with a mountain bike stem and handlebar combo. Competition led the way in bike development and by the end of the decade signature model bikes became available as stars were being born.

European manufacturers were also in on the game, producing bikes in great numbers, but the driving force behind development was the US. The company Specialized were one of the first to mass market complete off-the-shelf bikes with the Stumpjumper. This bike, based on the early Tom Ritchey frame, was hugely popular and still continues to be refined, even today. The industry as a whole learned a lot from the Tom Ritchey built bike, but Specialized had the research and design money to allow them to continue to play with the build parameters. Inevitably, people were influenced by other manufacturers' products, even if they were working away on their own small tweak or modification. Big players in the industry from the West worked closely with the industrial giants in the East to develop a series of standards for components – something that is still happening today. This period saw refinement, rather than huge innovation and creation. It was, after all, the birth of the modern mountain bike and it would take some time before walking followed crawling.

Taiwanese manufacturers were producing equipment at a rapid rate and the eighties saw a few interesting innovations that included oval chainrings and the U brake. Both of these products became hugely popular with manufacturers throughout this period. Anyone who used a U brake and rode in muddy conditions back then will appreciate just how things have

U-brakes were less effective than U-boats.

moved on. Rear ends and hub axle widths changed from 130mm to the current 135mm, and bottom bracket widths were established for the time being. I think this also indicates just how young the sport is – at the time it was hard to conceive what the future would bring. But to anyone comparing the standard of mountain bike engineering to developments made previously in automotive engineering, especially in motor sports, the future would have looked bright.

Racers demanded better equipment and top teams were working with manufacturers developing products to give their riders that competitive edge. This was a really healthy thing – the bikes were honestly not up to the job from a design point of view, and failures in forks, cranks and wheels were still commonplace, especially for a new hungry breed of rider who, like myself, had been inspired by those early pioneers. In the late eighties the introduction of aluminium bikes, and even the very rare and exotic titanium frames, would redefine hard-tail race bikes in the years to come. Geometry was being tweaked, and the engineers in companies (usually small and US-based) were experimenting with different fork designs and construction techniques.

As, at the time, riders had to battle it out in all disciplines to be crowned the best, the same bike was being ridden in the cross-country, uphill, downhill and trials. Aspiring riders would practise all the necessary skills and make modifications to their bikes to suit themselves. Handlebar extensions helped in the uphill and wider tyres with softer pressures would help in the trials. It was a baptism of fire and a real trial-and-error era, where concepts and products were coming and going at a rapid rate. Another decade was soon to pass, by which point mountain biking had taken off on a truly global scale.

>> THE NINETIES

As we rolled into the nineties, fashion trends started to change, in both the bikes and the clothes. The mass boom exposed some colourful characters to the scene and, like all recreational sports, mountain biking was developed, pushed and shaped by the players in the industry. When it comes to the faces you see in the media, that means the racers and riders. People were experimenting with different bike setups, handlebar shapes, bar extensions, chain devices and gear ratios as well as the obviously rapidly growing choice of tyres. Components manufactured using computer numerical control (CNC) were everywhere and in every colour imaginable.

An innovative replacement for cables. This component would fit between cantilever brakes and attach to the main brake cable.

Talk to anyone out there who rode in those days and I'm sure you'll find that they speak about riding back then like it was yesterday. There really

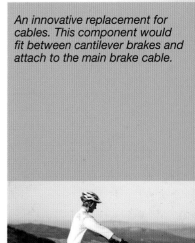

Failures were still frequent in the CNC era.

Braze-on for pannier racks sat side-by-side with seven speed.

were some fancy components and funky finishes to capture the eye and imagination. To go with the new gear, a new language was being born with old-school surf terminology being replaced by a multitude of words to describe the nature of this sport, now so deeply entwined with technology. A new generation of engineers would leave a mark in mountain bike history through the nineties. CNC-machined products by outfits like Ringle, Cooks Brothers, Chris King, Grafton Research and Paul's Components were on everyone's must-have list.

For me personally, this benchmark era was so exciting. I was starting to see the possibilities of just how far things could progress now that race-car style manufacturing techniques were being used. Sure, stuff still bent and broke, but less often than before. Let's be honest, when you look at top riders and what they do with the equipment, it's no wonder you have the odd failure!

But what about the overall bike package? Things were hotting up and the global industry was a lucrative place to be for any cycle manufacturer. Bikes now had better braking systems, although it was not until around 1994 that the V-style brake was introduced. These units were cable-operated but much more efficient than previous cantilevers, thanks to better lever and calliper design. Exotic bikes were being equipped with cartridge bearings where it counts, and manufacturing giant Shimano progressed essential items at a rapid rate.

Another innovation in the early nineties was the introduction of a mountain bike specific clip-in pedal – Shimano were at it again. For the racers and the recreational user, this advance in pedal technology was a huge leap forward. SPD clip-in pedals, or 'SPDs', made riding more efficient, and for the racers that all-important mounting and dismounting process sped up. Other manufacturers followed suit and creative methods of holding a cleat onto an axle were developed. Fancy pedals joined other shiny components that would catch your eye from a nicely lit glass counter in the local bike shop. Another manufacturer, Onza, produced a clip-in pedal system using elastomers as springs. Tom Ritchey was still in the game but now focused on producing quality components. Unlike some products from this era, SPDs, or 'spuds' as they became known, were here to stay.

Cross-country bikes started to branch off into different genres of mountain bike, although they were still very similar to each other. This was reflected through their geometry and construction material. Lightweight aluminium and titanium bikes were weighing in at as little as 20 pounds – that's just over 9 kilograms! These bikes were really race bikes – steeper angles in the head and seat tube and tighter rear triangles with shorter chainstay lengths created fast-handling, efficient bikes. Bike shops sold complete

setups now equipped with 24 gears. Some models boasted braze-ons (see Glossary) to hang pannier racks on for those who wanted to use their bike for expedition riding.

Sloping top tubes and more compact frame design came to the forefront, and innovations like the elevated chain stay appeared. Thankfully, round chainrings replaced traditional oval ones and drive-train components would soon go through a process of being shrunk. At this stage, though, riders competing in downhill were experimenting with larger and larger chainrings to increase the speed. Smaller chainrings and more compact components would not become available until the mid-nineties. Brakes had become streamlined and the overall look of components was slick and smooth.

By the mid-nineties, square-tapper bottom-bracket axles were being phased out for the new ISIS and Octalink standards with a round over-sized axle and a crank arm secured in place with a large bolt. These new units came whole with improved bearings and seals. Oversized splined axles and larger Allen bolts held lighter-weight hollow crank arms. Chainring sizes had settled to 28t, 38t and 48t split and the look was flush. The whole thing was a huge improvement on cup and cone. However, manufacturers still used the cup-and-cone system in hubs. Thanks to improved technology, better seals were being used and harder-wearing

New improved sealed units and splined axles paved the way.

internals now meant that the constant cleaning of your dirty bike did not destroy your hubs after two weeks.

Now the rare and exotic arrived – bicycle manufacturers American produced a frame fabricated from the metal beryllium, another US company, Kestral, were one of a few manufacturers selling carbon-fibre bikes, and even Lotus, the legendary sports-car manufacturer, produced a carbon monocoque front-ended cross-country race bike for top UK racer Deb Murrell.

The early nineties welcomed suspension. Downhill riders were hitting larger obstacles and travelling faster than before, and frame design had to move on accordingly. Dave Cullinan's famous victory at the 1992 World Championships in Bromont, Canada, marked the end of an era. This was the first time a full-suspension bike had been ridden to victory in the downhill – he even used clip-in pedals in the process. Never again would a hard-tail bike win the world championships in downhill.

Early full-suspension bikes were aimed at being all-round bikes and still utilised single-crown forks, with the exception of the Off Road brand. Their system of using elastomers as a suspension unit was hugely popular. Following the success of the Flex Stem (a handlebar stem that pivoted, compressing a small elastomer), the Girvin-bladed fork resembled that of a modern-day triple clamp. It used a parallelogram system for the fork to move through, compressing a vertically mounted elastomer. Hydraulic and air systems would dominate, however, and provided the best tunable method for suspending bikes and riders. Doug Bradbury, the man behind Manitou, was also machining some awesome components and using elastomer technology in his suspension units.

Companies played with different pivot placements for the optimum full-suspension bike. Their aim was to produce an efficient system that would not be affected by a rider's input through the pedals. Accordingly, the rider input ought not to affect the performance of the linkage and suspension unit. Early bikes utilised single-pivot designs before the new link system designed by Horst Leitner hit the scene. The unified triangle design was another favourite, although on higher quality bikes this design would also be dropped in the years to come. Brake jack – where braking lifts the rear wheel or locks out the suspension making it useless – and other undesired effects from braking forces also caused issues for designers and fabricators when building a full-suspension frame. At this time, mountain biking had not made the split into all the different genres we see today – bikes were still being used as all-round setups. For things to move forwards, a split in design was inevitable. Sometime around the mid-nineties, the first long-travel, big-hitting, slack-angled downhill bikes hit the scene. Once again another sector in the mountain bike market opened, and for the first time you could buy a specific downhill rig, but at a cost.

Full-suspension bikes were starting to adopt slacker angles and more compact frame design. The cross-country market thrived upon the developments being made in downhill. Suspension component parts were being machined to a much higher standard than before – efficiency and effectiveness started to be developed on a larger scale to suit the needs of the world's fastest racers and this engineering could simply be shrunk to fit the cross-country bikes. Riders now started to push the capabilities of the bikes further, venturing onto terrain that was just dream material a decade ago. A new free and aggressive cross-country style of riding was born. Not quite the free-ride you see now with guys and girls hucking 30m drops, but it is thanks to those early extreme heads that such things are achievable. With the advanced technology, boundaries were definitely being pushed.

Released in the mid-90s the M1 dominated the downhill scene for many years.

Once again the US were dominating the market with their design work. Only the Italians and Marzocchi could compete in quality and performance in the suspension fork market. Suffice to say, a huge percentage of all equipment was still being manufactured in the Far East, hence the desirable hand- and CNC-machined US parts became the Gucci of mountain biking. You start to get the idea of just how much development was made throughout this period – key components were being developed that are now considered everyday necessities. Small machine shops with their hand-crafted precision finish influenced the companies in the Far East. Every large corporation wanted a market share and, thanks to those backyard engineer shops, the corporations upped their game. Quality raw

materials and superior finishing were adopted by the eastern giants and superior equipment filtered down to the everyday consumer, ever curious to discover the pleasure of mountain biking.

European and Taiwanese wheel manufacturers crafted lighter and stronger rims. Mavic from France were dominant even then and this was the choice rim to spec on your trick setup. They developed ceramic-coated rims to improve the efficiency of cantilever and V brakes, and they had a reputation for building bomb-proof hoops, or wheel rims. Other companies produced lighter rims, but the weight-saving only paid dividends for a short period of time. Mavic's longevity in the industry is thanks to the longevity of their product. Ultimately, though, there is an element to every consumer market that buys into fashion rather than into function, and this leaves a nice hole in the rim market to be filled by smaller outfits producing different rim options.

Radial lacing helps reduce weight.

Through the nineties, people played with different spoke-lacing techniques, a fad that has fallen by the wayside, yet may one day have a revival. The favoured triple-cross method for lacing spokes was thrown to one side and radial-built lightweight wheels were being experimented with. Snowflake front wheels were also another twist (excuse the pun) on lacing techniques. To build a wheel like this, thinner spokes would be twisted around each other to increase their strength, which gave the final build a snowflake effect. This experimentation was also a sign that wheels were still frequently being rebuilt after buckling, denting or just wearing out on the braking surface. As always we still had room for improvement.

Another product worth mentioning is the Tioga Disc Drive – a composite rear disc wheel utilising Kevlar strands mounted in a carbon weave. The idea was not only to be more efficient through the air but also to allow the wheel to flex slightly, giving a little extra grip through its shock-absorbing technology. Later models used clear, wafer-thin plastic to suspend the Kevlar strands. This high-maintenance component made a sound to die for – an unmistakable hollow rumble filled the air as riders whizzed by, and you just knew the bike belonged in the kitsch must-have category.

By the mid-nineties, riser bars were being favoured by downhill and slalom riders, but most cross-country riders were still using flat bars, and still do so today. The fad of bar extensions – another product that made it big in the eighties through the likes of Onza and Answer – soon faded out. Only a few die-hard fans kept their bar extensions, which had by then shrunk in proportion, as had the demand. Yet more standards were being achieved as steerer tubes and headsets became oversized to 1⅛ inches. To go with the improved rigidity, stem design changed from the old-fashioned internal quill to a new external clamping system. Longer steerer tubes protruded from the top of the headset and stems clamped around this. The Aheadset became the system of choice for all manufacturers.

An early A-head stem by US manufacturer Control Tech.

Hydraulic-operated disc and rim brakes burst onto the scene, notably on the front fork produced by Mountain Cycle in the early nineties. This was an upside-down suspension fork, named the 'Suspenders', with a disc rotor and calliper mounted on each leg. Mountain Cycle's brakes looked awesome but, heavily CNC-machined and over-engineered by today's standards, they had the power but unfortunately also the weight to go with them. With cross-country riding still dominating the mass market,

Magura brakes are still in production today.

even the hardcore downhill riders were looking for light weight to go with the performance.

Rim brakes, using hydraulic systems, were readily available thanks to Magura from Germany, the only downside to these super-efficient units being the excessive rim-crushing stopping power and inefficient quick-release mechanism. Use a tyre larger than an inch and a half and you had to fiddle around with levers and remove half of the unit to get your wheel out. Early models had no quick-release at all, so the tyre had to be deflated to clear the brake when removing the wheel.

Hope Technology from the UK – a name most mountain bikers today are familiar with – revolutionised disc brakes in the mid-nineties. Sure, early models used to boil oil and fade out on super-long descents, but the guys from Yorkshire battled on, and in no time at all had developed solid units that were compact, lightweight and in demand from nations of eager mountain bikers. Early open systems were replaced by closed systems, and multiple piston designs were experimented with. You can still get four-pot disc brakes today and unfortunately they still suffer from inconsistent piston movement. I personally feel the volume of brake fluid is just too small to get these units working consistently. There is not enough of a vacuum inside to pull back all the piston evenly. Riders suffer from pads wearing out unevenly and that old noise of pad rubbing disc instead of wheel rim is evident. Multiple options of disc brake came about in the late nineties and industry standards for mounting hardware were born.

Tyre manufacturers had become another sector within the sport that joined in the arms race. It was inevitable that different types of tyre needed to be developed for different terrains. The late eighties saw the start of this movement but the nineties saw some large leaps forward in tyre technology. There was now a better understanding of the different terrain types that people were riding on across the globe. Huge amounts of trail miles had been covered and research continued. Different cuts (tyre tread patterns), compounds and build techniques were being played with and the consumer could choose from a vast array. Racers had the luxury of special tyres to indulge in, but only a few of these prototypes would make production stage. It would be some time yet before the general public had soft compound rubber available at the click of a mouse.

For the purist, this period was so exciting, but it did not pass without its problems. The image of mountain biking was being tainted by cheap imports and bikes that were obviously not fit for purpose. Companies all over the globe were requesting mountain bikes at affordable prices for the masses, and bikes were being sold branded as 'Mountain Bikes' or 'All Terrain Bikes' that just simply would not cut it out on the trail. Sure, it got people into riding who might progress to buying a real mountain bike, lovingly developed and meticulously designed and manufactured, but the failure rate of equipment not only put some folk off the sport but also potentially endangered their lives.

Twelve-inch suspension bikes became available in the late nineties but in very small numbers. The limited success rate of dropping huge banks and getting away with it was reflected in the sales figures. These bikes were intended for one thing – the huge suspension and over-built nature of the frames equalled huge weight and poor pedal efficiency. Downhill racers chose to use bikes in the six to eight inch range, and in the later part of the decade, Rock Shox from the US released the first generation of Boxxer downhill forks. They featured eight inches of travel with adjustable compression and rebound, giving you a fully tunable fork.

For a while, the well-known US brand Specialized, along with a few other manufacturers, played with 24-inch rear wheels. They were once again using their huge R&D department and influencing the smaller manufacturers in the process. The smaller 24-inch wheels spun up faster but would not roll over rough ground so well. The trade-off and phase soon passed. For most people in the sport, 26-inch wheels were the preferred choice. Urban riding seemed to be the only area where a smaller wheel choice was beneficial.

Urban riding and dirt jumping were on the rise in the mid-nineties. Mountain bikers who were inspired by the BMX scene took their stock bikes into new terrain and started building and riding street spots and dirt jumps. Again, technology was pushed to its limits as riders used bikes beyond their purpose, and failures were frequent. This mirrored the progression made by the Klunkerz of Marin county in the sixties and seventies, as they too took bikes designed for a very different purpose out into uncharted territory. They went from trail riding to downhill racing, and in the process exposed the weakness in the equipment – just another case of history repeating itself?

There was an obvious need and opportunity within the sport for yet another new type of mountain bike frame design. This new craze would be hugely beneficial to the sport on many levels, as old-school riders had a new toy to play with – the by-product of which meant new skills were being gained and essential trail skills progressed. Manufacturers tapped into a new market, and kids in urban areas benefited from having the option to ride a bike and challenge themselves on a personal level and in a positive way. A new career option was in the pipeline.

Frame builders steepened up the head angles and fitted rigid or short-travel suspension forks. They cut horizontal rear dropouts and riders chose to use stronger oversized BMX cranks for strength; billet stems machined from one block, and narrow riser bars finished off the clean-looking simplistic builds. Urban riding was taken to a new level, as the

Tight single tracks require pinpoint accuracy for wheel placement.

The Spooky Bandwagon.

Slimmer cogs on the 9-speed cassette.

simple design and tough construction of the bikes enabled riders to repeat manoeuvres that would have previously damaged their all-rounder cross-country bikes. Daring lines would put you one step ahead of the competition and the scene flourished as riders pushed the boundaries. People were taking lines and riding features that replicated things you might find in an everyday trail ride or dream trail. The smooth curves of skateboarding and snowboarding fused with the ability to roll along on a huge variety of surfaces, creating infinite lines to the creative mind.

So much happened in the nineties – companies grew and, unfortunately for some, died in the early nineties economic downturn. We owe to the rare and exotic machines of that era the affordability and quality of components available today. There were so many innovative companies and products that I could have mentioned in this section, and they all played a part in progressing the sport.

>> THE NOUGHTIES

We enter the next millennium and mountain bike engineering continues to develop at a steady rate. There are a multitude of frame styles now being fine-tuned for each discipline that has evolved. Manufacturers are still modifying linkage systems on both downhill free-ride and cross-country frames, but most of the critical development here has been done. Shock manufacturers will play a major role in moving the sport on throughout this decade as more research is done through world cup racing.

Hydro-forming is a process where the tube is extruded using water jets in a centrifuge – this eliminates imperfections in the tube and it is the new CNC. Once again Specialized, Trek and Giant lead the way with high-quality mass-production mountain bikes. The consumer has never had it so good, with high-grade high-spec bikes being produced in vast numbers. The value for money compared to early top-end bikes is phenomenal. Off-the-shelf bikes are built with components any kid growing up in the eighties would have died for. Luckily for them and the industry, they have both come of age. Any hardcore enthusiast is now in a position to buy their own high-spec bike right off the shelf or via the ever-expanding world wide web.

So let's take a look at the refined bikes and the different genres that we'll cover in Chapters 4 and 5.

- Cross-country trail and race bikes

- Short-travel full-suspension: 80–120 mm

- Dirt jump (DJ) and street bikes

- Trials bikes

- Medium-travel/cross-country and all-mountain: 120–160 mm

- Long-travel/all-mountain and free-ride: 160–180 mm

- Long-travel/downhill and free-ride: 180 mm+

Stock bikes were now becoming so well spec'd that the value for money, compared to a decade ago, was fantastic. An off-the-shelf full-suspension cross-country bike could be picked up for as little as £700. Compare this to a setup from 10 years before and things looked pretty good for the consumer. The US were once again at the forefront, pushing the boundaries and influencing the East to produce products to suit. Slope style and free-ride were born, and the craze of dropping huge cliffs and gap jumps had arrived. A new breed of rider adopted the bike and new fashions followed.

The year 2001 saw the Red Bull Rampage competition – a free-ride comp that was judged on points as opposed to time. The Rampage inspired riders and the years that followed would see them go further – dropping larger and larger cliffs. Rumour has it the competition was stopped because things were getting out of hand. Failure to ride out clean from a drop would leave riders badly beaten up and lucky to be alive. Later in

5th Element rear shock absorber with and without coil spring.

the decade, the Crankworx competition and festival would fill the extreme free-ride competition hole left by the Rampage.

Innovation continued and the turn of the century welcomed nine speed. Slimmer chains gave a wider spread of gear ratios – this trend would enable riders to opt for running two chainrings. Middleburn from the UK released a crank set that allowed just two rings to be fitted – a brave move, and an option that would become more popular in the years that followed.

Gear ratios had dropped from the early nineties craze of monster chainrings to a smaller compact 24t, 34t, 44t split and anything from an 11- to 34-tooth cog was achievable on the rear cassette (the cluster of cogs on the rear hub body). Chain devices had developed into high-quality precision items and frame builders included braze-ons for the device of choice. International standards for the mounting to the frame were appearing and would change little before the end of the decade.

Elastomer suspension was finally dropped by all major suspension manufacturers and oil- and air-damped systems were being tweaked. A big step for all rear shock absorbers was the adaptation of an internal valving system used in dune buggies and desert race cars. To control the yule on a buggy internal, valving could be dialled in to control small bumps and make the suspension more or less active. The company 5th Element produced shock absorbers for motor sports and were the first people to bring this adjustable internal valving to mountain bikes. Overnight, bike stability and on-the-fly adjustability revolutionised aggressive cross-country riding. The advance opened up the possibility to build longer-travel bikes – these bigger-hitting cross-country bikes could deal with more aggressive terrain downhill and still climb efficiently uphill. Other manufacturers of shock absorbers would develop their own systems and improve on the early 5th Element design. Now, like most component parts, shock absorbers came in standard lengths and widths so the never-ending ability to upgrade your stock off-the-shelf bike continued.

Ten-inch-travel mountain bikes were now in production stage but they never sold in huge quantities. The good all-round cross-country bike and the urge to cruise along a trail dominated sales statistics. The risks associated with the other disciplines for most people just didn't outweigh the accessibility and fun factor gained from cross-country riding. The sport would soon enter the Olympics, a sign of its epic proportions. No longer an underground scene, mountain biking had hit the mainstream big time. Every day, new people started taking to the hills in search of thrills and the odd spill.

As bikes got better sprung, riders were hitting things at greater speeds and with greater force. Wheels, sets and rim designs were still being modified, putting paid to that old saying about reinventing the wheel. Downhill racers demanded better rim sets and a solution to the never-ending problem of pinch or 'snakebite' punctures – where the tyre contacts the rim and the tube is 'pinched' in between the tyre and rim. The solution would be yet another piece of technology developed in the automotive world. Tubeless-specific rims and tyres started to appear on racers' bikes and were soon available to the consumer. The systems were more expensive, however, and most people left them for the top racers and the affluent.

I often hear banter about the advantages and disadvantages of the systems but I myself opt for the tubeless system. Early setups used to be a pain – the tyres were awkward to fit and they did not seal like today's versions. As with most things in life, a bit of time and patience pays dividends and I no longer suffer from snakebite punctures. Sure, you can still rip the sidewall out on sharp rocks, but just carry the right equipment and your ride will continue – it's no different from getting a flat with the old inner tube system.

Tubeless rims are stronger as they are not drilled out for spoke lancing.

Some sweet tweaks to existing products made life that little bit better. It's amazing how the little things are taken for granted by new-school riders and yet the old school marvel at their simplicity and ingenuity. Lock-on grips are such a simple concept but benefit us in many ways. No more buying new grips or suffering moving grips on wet days. Just undo the Allen bolts and slide off. I have the pleasure of staying up all night working as a mechanic for my teammates at 24-hour race events. A busy pit, running up to five riders, each using two bikes, gets that bit more hectic when you have multiple repairs to attend to: a bent brake or gear lever may need repairing, or even a set of bars could be damaged and need replacing, in a Formula One style pit stop. For most people lock-on grips are safer and easier to fit, making them a first choice.

Shimano's replacement pin on the left and the SRAM quick-link on the right. Better than sliced bread.

A simple piece of equipment like a chain can be improved upon and has been over the years. Chain links and methods of joining chains together have existed in many different forms for a long time. Shimano had been using a profiled chain with their patented Hyperglide system since the late eighties. Their preferred method for joining new chains still consists of a joining pin that is longer than necessary. Push the pin through until it clicks in place then snap off the excess – a system that produces a very strong joint, but the downside comes when you are in a situation where the chain breaks and you need a fast fix. Rejoining chains by pushing pins typically leaves a weak or stiff joint; it's also a tricky job when you are cold or in a hurry. The solution developed by SRAM, an American bicycle component manufacturer, was the creation of a pair of links with one pin in each at opposite ends. The pins have small grooves in them that locate

into the slots on each other and click into place. This system is fast and very effective.

Internal headsets entered the frame – larger diameter bearing cups sat inside flared-head tubes. Using the internal system allows riders to get the bar height down, putting more weight over the front end, increasing grip. There is a trade-off and a sweet spot where the front end becomes either too high or too low. For this reason there is still a market for external systems. Frame and fork builders would use oversize 1½-inch steerer tubes in downhill setups and, in the latter part of the decade, cross-country bikes started to adopt 1½-inch lower bearing race with 1⅛-inch upper bearing race for extra rigidity and superior steering capabilities.

The simplicity of the internal head-set.

Sealed cartridge bearings and dust covers keep the elements out.

Crank sets were still morphing and changing in design aesthetic. Many manufacturers developed systems similar to the Bull's Eye crank set seen in the late eighties. Superior manufacturing techniques have created the ability to produce crank sets that are lighter and easier to install and maintain. The system consists of one crank arm being integrated with the axle. Oversized bearings would become mounted externally to the bottom bracket shell. The opposing crank arm slides onto splines and is held into place with a retention bolt.

Another concept would emerge in the drive-train department as manufacturers started to develop gear boxes for downhill bikes. Nicolai and Honda both developed systems consisting of internal drive mechanisms. Later, sneak shots revealed the Honda box to contain standard drive components cased in aluminium and carbon, with a Honda mod or two. The Nicolai internals closely resemble that of a car gear box, with multiple machined drive components changing the ratio at which the crank axle spins. The problem any gear box suffers is friction. Huge advances have been made to reduce this, but the external drive system is still favoured by the mainstream.

Geared hubs had been in development for some time. Rohloff are well known in the industry for producing solid units that seem to go on for ever and ever. The only downside to gear hubs is the weight. Located behind the centre of the bike, gear hubs tend to make a bike rear-heavy, whereas locating the hub (or specific G'Box) in the bottom bracket region affects the handling far less, and the weight remains centred and low. Hub gear systems could be the future for those of us who have to deal with harsh winter conditions. There are fewer components to wear out, and mud, grime and other material that would normally effect a drive chain are no longer a bother, with all the key moving parts being encased by the hub body. Will we see top-end options available in the years to come?

As in the previous decade, backyard engineers continued to develop innovative bikes. Alan Millyard from the UK produced a bike billed to change the way manufacturers look at drive and suspension systems. His background in aerospace and military engineering, and not bicycles, brought a breath of new life. Approaching the problem from this different angle, a clear vision gave him the idea to encase all the drive components into the rear monocoque. He reduced the width of the rear axle by mounting a Shimano gear hub in the front monocoque, driven off the cranks. By removing the exposed rear derailleur, riders could take tighter lines through rocks and stumps. Even if they were to hit something it would not affect the drive and ability to finish a run down the hill. He also asked some interesting questions as to why people set up their bikes so stiff, measuring rebound and compression in environments unlike those they would be used in. The great suspension debate continues.

Single-speed bikes made a comeback in the noughties. Companies produced single-speed specific frames, as another scene develops within a scene. People will always want to challenge themselves and riding the same trails with one gear ratio is another way of doing it. This was the first time that mountain bike engineering took a backwards step. The simplicity and silence of a single speed is a reflection of consumer trends in the 21st century with regard to design. Minimalism had engulfed mountain biking as mankind found satisfaction in simplicity.

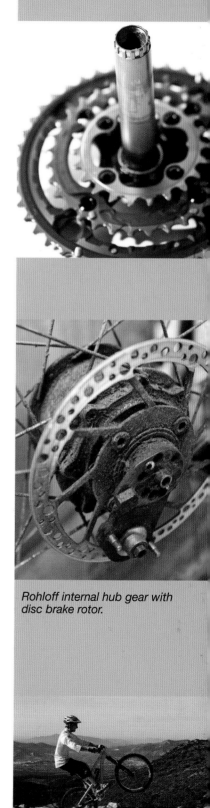

Rohloff internal hub gear with disc brake rotor.

Single speed with horizontal drop-out.

While some of the cross-country riders made things more simple, the downhill riders still required technology to assist them. Bolt-through axles became standard affairs on front forks in the late nineties. Stiffer than quick-release mechanisms, oversize 20mm front axles give better steering response. By removing the flex in the lower fork leg, a bike turns in and tracks far better. Cross-country riders have also started to adopt lightweight versions. Rear bolt-through designs and the introduction of wider 150mm rear ends soon followed. Once again the frames became stiffer and suffered little in the way of excess weight, thanks to the use of aircraft-spec materials. However, all these oversize components added together had taken the weight of a downhill race bike from around 28 pounds in the mid-nineties to a staggering 40-odd pounds in the noughties.

The good old-fashioned wheel would be reinvented again as the US introduced the world to its twenty-niners (29ers) concept. Larger 29-inch diameter wheels roll over rough ground easier but do suffer from increased centrifugal force at higher speeds, making them harder to manoeuvre, especially on tight trails. This trend would be adopted by a few cross-country riders, but tyre manufacturers focused development and production on the industry-standard 26-inch versions. The need to buy a whole new frame to upgrade your wheel set and limited tyre choice would mean that only a few riders adopted 29ers.

Throughout the mid-noughties, downhill riders adopted wider bars and flat crowns for triple-clamp forks. A rider's torso is lowered when their hands are spread further apart and wider bars give more stability at speed. The lower flat crown helps, but the effect is marginal compared to increasing the bar width. When any adjustments to a rider's stance are made it is not without compromise. The wide-bar trend would benefit particular build types and bike geometries but not others. Sometimes it's an expensive process swapping equipment just to see how it feels – if done in a methodical fashion, however, it can be a very advantageous thing to do. You only really learn through direct experience, so it is critical to understand riding through feeling.

Wide bars are all the rage with downhill riders.

As the decade came to an end, SRAM introduced the first mountain bike 10-speed drive train, aimed at top cross-country race teams and riders who want something a little special. The system utilises an even narrower chain and a slimmer cassette. Upgrade components were boasting lighter weights and increased strength, and frame geometry had once again been changed but only ever so slightly. Since the nineties, top-tube lengths had shrunk slightly on mid-travel bikes but hard-tails remained pretty much the same. Classic models like the GT Zaskar and Marin Bear Valley remain firm favourites among riders. Downhill bikes have seen small revisions and US manufacturer Diamond Back have gearbox bikes readily available for the masses.

Rear mechanisms by Shimano; the DCD chain retention roller; and Early Hope front hub with centre locking ring for the disc rotor.

RECREATIONAL RIDING_

As we have seen in previous chapters, mountain biking's popularity has gone from strength to strength. The industry thrives and more people are taking to the hills for recreational pleasure. The racers at the top end drive forward the technological development of the equipment and the consumer benefits from their efforts. In return the investment that people make in their bikes and equipment is being pumped back into R&D. This never-ending cycle has created more than just jobs in bike shops – mountain biking is a serious career option for any young person venturing out into the world of work. Once just a recreational pastime, mountain biking soon became a sport, but as it grew in popularity through the eighties the recreational element would still be the breadwinner for most manufacturers. With so many people out riding trails, it was inevitable that at some point there would be the need for facilities and control measures for the recreational user.

The International Mountain Bike Association (IMBA) was created in the US in 1988 by a group of Californian mountain bike clubs. They could see the conflict between the different trail user groups starting to occur and wanted to demonstrate that mountain bikes that were ridden responsibly had little impact on trails and surrounding wildlife. IMBA continues to liaise between different countryside user groups in an effort to promote mountain biking in a positive way. Volunteer groups help create new trail networks and maintain existing ones, and the organisation works on a global scale alongside land managers and other trail user groups. Over the years IMBA has grown in strength and is represented in more than 40 countries. The sport owes a lot to the foresight that those guys and girls in California had in the late eighties.

Today there are many fringe outfits that work alongside IMBA – all helping to develop new standards in trail building and in the provision of specific trail centres, or 'bike parks' as they are otherwise known, for people to enjoy. Mountain biking is taken seriously, as it should be, by local authorities across the globe. Recreational users bring huge revenue to rural economies and, out of all the countryside user groups, mountain bikers are top of the tree when it comes to spending per head. For this reason, we have seen huge growth in trail building, attracting riders to far-flung corners of the globe in search of the perfect ride. Major ski

Riding natural trails is all about line choice.

resorts have adapted their lift systems to accommodate the bikers, and the quiet summer months of these places continue to get busier. New business opportunities have been created and certificates of professional competency can be achieved in guiding and teaching and will be available soon in trail building. All over the globe local authorities are capitalising on the benefits mountain biking can bring.

>> THE INFLUENCE OF THE TRAIL CENTRE

Way-marked shared trails had existed for some time in various locations before specific, purpose-built bike-only trails appeared. Penshurst Off-Road Club in Kent built a site on private land for the purpose of mountain biking back in 1990, but it was father and son Mike and Ian Warby from Firecrest who developed one of the first mountain bike specific trail networks in the UK on public land at Aston Hill. This land was, up until this point, managed by the government body Forestry Commission England, and Mike and Ian could see the benefits of working with them to establish a network of trails where riders could ride with no worries of meeting oncoming traffic and other trail users. They had a vision and took a gutsy move to push mountain biking in an area that previously banished bikes back to boring muddy bridleways.

Aston Hill was the pioneering centre that paved the way for sustainable, financially viable mountain bike specific sites in the UK. By creating an area dedicated to bikes, the Warbys could coach riders and introduce newbies to the fun there was to be had on two knobby tyres. Ian coached his first group of customers in 1998 and has since coached hundreds of riders. The 45-hectare forest had a cross-country loop marked out by Mike in 1990. This was followed by a specific downhill track in 1996 and a four-cross (4X) track soon after, giving people a place to ride and measure their performance in relative safety.

Other trails were being created in north Wales by Dafydd Davis at Coed Y Brenin, a location that became hugely popular in the late nineties. Once again Dafydd worked in partnership with the Forestry Commission to create hard-wearing purpose-built trails for mountain bikes only. The creators of Penshurst, Aston Hill and Coed Y Brenin all deserve a place in the mountain bike Hall of Fame. The last two definitely changed the Forestry Commission's view on mountain biking and paved the way for other trail centres to be built in the UK. Yet again, a new phase of recreational mountain biking was born.

There are many forms of mountain biking, all of which can be done at a recreational level. The trend of bike parks would grow throughout the next decade, and large ski resorts, like Whistler in Canada and Les Getz in France, invested large sums of money to create off-season/low-season networks of trails that could be monitored and maintained to a high standard. Forestry Commission Scotland could also see the benefits of investing in mountain biking and, following the tragic foot and mouth disaster that wiped out huge amounts of livestock and closed down much of the countryside for recreation, they created the 7stanes project. The aim of the project was simple: they wanted to give tourism a jump start after foot and mouth. I have been fortunate to have an input in creating some of the features at 7stanes centres.

Forestry Commission Scotland set about creating seven centres of excellence across southern Scotland, building trails to a high standard that would be sustainable for years to come. Each centre would have trails of different grades and facilities to support them. The investment paid off and Scotland has been voted by IMBA as the best destination in the world for a mountain biking holiday for two years running. Many new business opportunities have been created and the visitor numbers continue to rise each year. The trails themselves have been built to such a high standard that people from all over the world come to meet the creators and learn how to recreate such a well-built, robust trail.

Trail centres may not be everyone's cup of tea but they do have their place in mountain biking. I personally think that it's thanks to them that the recreational element of the sport has grown so much over the years. They seem to fill a void in mountain biking, making it more accessible to

Narrow log rides and boardwalks help riders pass over boggy terrain.

A built trail in Scotland.

A recycling bike wash. All the minerals are collected and returned to nature.

Infrastructure is imperative, signage being a key component.

everyday people – very much in keeping with our 21st-century consumer lifestyle. The idea that you can go for an hour's blast after work on a red route (*see* grading system below), simply following the arrows, is a sign of our need to have the arduous things done for us.

Trail centres fit in nicely with the package-holiday mentality – the hassle-free system of having everything (other than the pedalling) done for you. You no longer need to read a map to navigate a ride on trails that may or may not be fun and flowing – the theme park roller-coaster nature of purpose-built trails guarantees a quality no-nonsense ride with fun features that will inevitably put a smile on your face. They are a great place to measure performance and give people that urge to improve. Trail features can be repeated lap after lap and well-built trails change little compared to natural trails with regard to erosion from the elements.

The downside to this type of trail is the lack of technicality to the riding. Built trails are just that – built. They have a design element to them that natural trails do not. I often teach people who will happily ride a black-grade section but, when put into relatively easy natural terrain, they struggle with it – the main reason being that it's not been built to flow. Natural trails rarely have that synchronistic fit between wheel and earth – you have to work harder to make the bike flow through them. It seems everything is opposing you rather than aiding you. Creative line choice is an essential component to making them flow, and this creative line choice is removed on purpose-built trails. Most riders develop the habit of following the worn groove or smooth line. Only short sections of purpose-built trails require line choice, whereas the huge majority of natural trails need the constant adjustment and creation of it.

>> WHERE ARE WE?

Another key skill is being lost in our modern age thanks to GPS and way-marked infrastructures. Map reading is a key skill to all old-school riders and an essential one at that. The ability to navigate from features in nature and from grid references is a fine art and a very fulfilling one too. Once the skill has been mastered, the world becomes a huge playground. No longer are you confined to the trail centre but you are able to find the most amazing views and trails. Exploration may not be on everyone's agenda but this form of recreational cycling is thankfully still very popular today.

My colleagues on the Syncros Endurance race team have taken mountain biking back to the mountains with their Seven Deadly Spins project. They set out to create new standards in endurance riding and have taken on several challenges to ride ancient routes in the UK in sub-24 hours, unsupported. By the time you read this, all the routes will have been recorded for you to go to enjoy at your own leisure. The idea was simple, but achieving it? Well, that's another story…

Purpose built trails are great training grounds. Rob Lee used such trails in preparation for his victory at the 2005 24-hour World Championship Race.

Over the years many people have set themselves exploratory and endurance-based challenges. The invention of the pedal cycle opened up even more possibilities for wilderness adventures. Modern bikes and equipment allow people to go further into the wilderness and, for some, to go faster in the process. I highly recommend grabbing a map and compass, learning the appropriate skills and getting out there to see what you can find.

Natural terrain offers multiple ride line options.

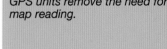

GPS units remove the need for map reading.

Guided rides are a great way to see new places.

>> GO ON, GET A GUIDE

As we have discovered, there are many new businesses riding on the success of mountain biking. Guided rides are hugely popular, with many companies offering holiday packages that include accommodation to go with a guide. This is a wonderful middle-ground option between navigating your own route and riding a trail centre. A good guide is worth every penny. With limited time on your vacation, removing the task of navigating in a foreign land allows you to get on with the all-important task of riding sweet trails.

I highly recommend seeking out a guide when travelling abroad, or to an area you are unfamiliar with. Make sure they are qualified to a recognised standard and carry the appropriate certification. A good guide will lead you on an interesting route suitable for your skill level and fitness – they will make a ride challenging but not too arduous. Guides are also trained to deal with any mechanical issues that may arise, so you can focus on enjoying your ride, knowing you will not be left up the proverbial creek without a paddle should something go wrong. All in all, a guide can bring a lot of value to your mountain biking experience.

There are a multitude of guide books out there that will point you in the right direction for locating mountain bike specific resorts. In the UK alone, there are in the region of 60 different sites with mountain bike specific trails, at all levels of difficulty, to challenge the recreational rider. As trail centres developed, there arose an obvious need for signage to guide riders and indicate the grades of trails. The piste system from skiing has been adopted by most countries to give a rough idea as to whether a trail is suitable for a rider's ability, but like most grading systems this is interpreted by designers and riders from the local vicinity and is not necessarily consistent between centres. So far the UK is the only country to have a standardised system of grading thanks to 99% of trails being on Forestry Commission managed land.

Holiday companies will entertain you both on and off the bike. Here a group enjoy dinner in the garden of Bike Village in the French Alps.

>> THE GRADING SYSTEM EXPLAINED

When grading trails, designers consider the following points:

- Elevation
- Inclination
- Width
- Exposure to the elements
- Distance
- Technical features/severity of terrain

Grade	Description
Green	Very easy, short routes with minimal exposure, usually on wide forest roads with good surfaces. In the UK, these routes are aimed at families.
Blue	Easy routes, slightly longer in distance than green trails. They include purpose-built, single-track sections and their width is narrower, typically around 1.2m. The exposure and gradients are slightly harder.
Red	Trails built for experienced riders. They contain technical features, including jumps, berms (banked corners) and north shore. There is more exposure to gradient and distance than on blue trails.
Black	Narrow and steep with lots of technical features. Black trails are aimed at seasoned mountain bikers. They typically head out into back country/remote locations and are more severe than red trails.
Black double diamond	Black trails having increased exposure to large drops and fall lines. These sections are for seasoned riders who want to go that bit further and challenge their nerve and technique.
Orange	Orange grading from snowboarding parks adopted by free-ride, slope style, north shore and jump parks. You will encounter raised wooden trails, having jumps with gaps that you have to commit to and can't roll through. These trails are intended for the very experienced rider.

Choose the correct grade trail and have fun.

>> A DIFFERENT TYPE OF CLUBBING

Another way to discover the pleasure of riding in the countryside is to join an established cycling club. Traditional road clubs often have a mountain bike branch to them, where you will find a friendly welcome and usually a cup of tea waiting for you. Cycling clubs organise weekly rides and trips away; they can help you with many aspects of your riding and are a great place to make new friends and shoot the breeze. Online forums are abundant and also another good source of information. Riders will pass on tips about good spots to ride and, again, will point you in the right direction to find trails appropriate to your needs. Just make sure you don't get glued to your monitor all day, chatting about bikes instead of riding them.

There is inevitably an element of trial and error required to pin down rides that float your boat. For me this is one of the great things about riding – awesome trails are far more rewarding to ride after having gone through the process of eliminating the not-so-good ones. The more experience you gain at riding different terrains, the better tuned your senses become to picking out areas that will yield good riding.

You may not have a club in your area, so starting one could be beneficial to riders where you live and also to the local economy. A club that is affiliated with a governing body can offer riders many benefits, from third-party insurance policies to discounts on a range of products. Local authorities will happily work with a recognised organisation and assist in acquiring funding for various projects, from after-school skills sessions to the creation of new trails and urban riding spots. Your club could help inspire the next generation to take to the trails. All the relevant information is available online and you will find some useful links in the appendix to this book. Just remember, the scene relies on people with energy and initiative to grow – I was inspired by that Californian scene and my mission in life is to pass on that knowledge so that there is a future.

>> THE NIGHT IS CALLING

Out of all the many types of mountain biking available to us, one of my favourite forms is recreational riding at night, which adds a whole new dimension to off-road exploration. A new world awaits us in the night as old well-ridden routes take on a different form. Lighting technology has progressed so much over the years and modern compact units make it possible to explore the wilderness in relative safety. You will encounter new challenges as your lights cast shadows on the trail, and bar-mounted lights often point in the wrong direction as you roll along, up and over trail features. A good addition to your night-riding kit is a helmet-mounted light. This enables you to spot landings, look through turns and illuminate those shady zones. With lower temperatures likely, take extra clothing and spare batteries or lights for those longer rides. The steady increase in 24-hour and 12-hour race events has meant that many people are taking on the challenge and enjoying the buzz these epic events give.

A helmet mounted light will help fill in those shady areas created by a larger more powerful handlebar mounted unit.

>> DIRT JUMPING, 4X AND BEYOND

Bike parks have seen the benefit of creating practice zones and specific features to suit the many forms of biking. The craze of dirt jumping has grown in popularity since the mid-nineties. I admit it's not everyone's first choice, but the market is large enough for manufacturers to produce a wide variety of bikes, all of them ready to hit the trails out of the shop. Dirt jump bikes are simple and versatile – they have compact frames, low knobby tyres and short travel forks. They are not dissimilar to street and 4X bikes and will see enough trail mileage to make them a choice investment.

With the sport fragmenting into so many different genres, it would seem the only way to tackle the different types of riding is to own and ride the

Various opportunities for jumps.

different types of bike. Where we used to ride one bike for all modern trail and course situations, the bike design has gone way beyond this. For instance, a cross-country race bike is not intended for throwing around skate parks and floating between jumps in a rhythm pack, nor would you expect it to perform well and stay in one piece down a world cup downhill track. Choosing the right bike is all-important for you in getting the most out of a discipline. There really is no one bike for the job – you will always compromise something when choosing a particular ride.

>> DOWNHILL

The use of chairlifts and uplifts has opened up remote terrain for recreational use and competition alike. Downhill-only riding is hugely popular and this element of the industry is comparable to Formula One. The technology in your everyday car has filtered down from top-level motor sport – the same goes for your everyday mountain bike and associated equipment. Those of you in the mountain bike scene have the advantage of being able to essentially buy a Formula One bike off the shelf. You will, however, encounter a price tag matching the scale of hill your rig is capable of taking on, if this is your chosen pastime. Fortunately, there are some more affordable options out there that are capable of dealing with similar terrain, and thanks to consumer demand most of us can opt for buying a six-inch-travel or full-on eight-inch-travel bike (without having to remortgage the house…).

Resorts and bike parks have a multitude of trails built with gravity in mind – look around for your local spot and you may be able to hire out a bike and give it a try before you commit your hard-earned money to a gravity-fed monster. The downside to this type of riding is how technically proficient you need to be to do it safely. Like all disciplines, the required skills can be perfected in safe environments, but you will inevitably have to put yourself out there to progress at the upper end.

The seasons for chairlift access are often limited, but some countries have uplift facilities that run for most of the year. The system of transporting you and your bike will vary from country to country, depending on their rules and regulations. Here in the UK, bikes and riders are separated – the bikes are stacked in trucks, while the riders are driven to the top of the hill in a coach. My good friend and trail riding buddy Tally is committed to the cause and he runs his uplift service in the Scottish Borders on a weekly basis. Thanks to guys like Tally, event organisers also benefit from a well-oiled professional service that makes their event possible. New Zealand remains at the forefront of extreme adventure, offering the opportunity to go Heli Biking. Over there, bikes and riders are helicoptered out into the mountains on a regular basis to access remote terrain.

>> URBAN RIDING

Urban exploration is growing in popularity with many riders. Towns and city councils are adopting the bike as governments make a big push to combat climate change. Cycle routes are popping up everywhere and, although it is not essentially mountain biking, they do offer the opportunity to get out in the fresh air and spin your legs. The creative element in your mind can easily turn a curb or drain lid into a trail feature, and you will discover views and places that you may not have been aware of. Here in the UK, there is a lot of investment being pumped into urban riding spots, with jumps and pump tracks popping up in town and city centre locations. They are a great resource, and riding them can improve your trail skills no end. Remember, there is no substitute for time on the bike.

There are many places to brush up on your riding technique in urban environments. Just make sure you are courteous to other people and obey the law of the land. To avoid any conflict, you may want to find your nearest BMX track or skate park. Most private parks have dedicated days or sessions for bikes, and public parks are often bike-friendly. They are great places to ride, offering a multitude of features that are similar to the types of obstacle you are likely to come across at a trail centre.

Skate parks are great places to play, the shape of the transitions are similar to those you will find out on the trail.

A basic day pack with the essential components.

>> BEFORE YOU GO OUT BLAZING TRAILS

When time is of the essence, we often neglect certain important criteria before hitting the trail or jump spot. Injuries often occur due to a lack of attention and care towards ourselves and our equipment. Cold muscles can be damaged by jumping on the bike and grinding up that inevitable first climb without having warmed up, and the same goes for taking a chairlift and rattling down a huge descent. Our bodies are fantastic machines, capable of producing immense performances, but like machines they eventually wear out.

To help avoid wearing out the component parts of the body and gain some longevity from our riding, it is vital to warm up at the start of every ride and warm down at the end. To back up the good work of exercise, we also need to keep hydrated and nourished. You will feel much better in your everyday life having exercised and released endorphins into the system, and better still if you replenish the nutrients used throughout this exchange. Get to know yourself and work with the body rather than against it. If you have strained a muscle or just got over the flu, you should consider whether going out on the bike is the right thing to be doing. Other, more gentle, forms of exercise can benefit your riding and you do not even need to leave your house to do them. Yoga, Tai Chi and similar practices all help focus the mind and increase your core strength. These gentle forms of exercise should at first be performed under the guidance of an expert to make sure you are using good technique and not opening up the possibilities of further injury.

To back up the exercise and good eating, I highly recommend you have your body serviced once in a while. Dysfunction in the body can impede your performance and well-being. Even day-to-day tasks have an impact on the skeletal and muscle structure of the body, and repetitive strain injuries are commonplace in fast-paced 21st-century living. I visit big Dave, my chiropractor/physiotherapist, and Dr Ju, my acupuncturist, at regular intervals throughout the year, and they both help to keep my body in tip-top condition. It's thanks to them that I am still capable of competing at a high level after punishing my body for over two decades.

Think about your body like your car. The car gets booked into a garage for routine inspections and work is carried out accordingly in relation to its wear and tear. The body is no different – so don't wait for the oil light to come on before checking the oil. Why wait for muscles to cramp and dysfunction to happen when routine maintenance can help to eliminate these problems? Use the best fuel and book those services at sensible intervals to get more out of your riding and your general day-to-day experiences.

◎ EQUIPMENT CHECKLIST

Depending on your chosen ride/discipline, you will need to tailor your equipment accordingly. Here is an overview of the things you should have with you when out riding.

- Suitable, well-maintained bike.

- Helmet that is the correct size, adjusted to fit properly in accordance with the manufacturer's recommendations. This should be in good condition and be fit for the purpose. For example, it is wise to use a full-face helmet for downhill riding.

- Well-fitted suitable clothing, including gloves and padded protection where required. Once again tailor this to suit your needs. Always ride in appropriate clothing for the terrain and surrounding environment.

In your hydration pack:

- Hydration – preferably water, although you may wish to use energy-enhancing additives.

- Spare inner tube – make sure you have the correct valve for your wheel type. I recommend using the Presta valves as they will fit all wheels.

- Tyre levers – the plastic versions are lighter and friendlier to tubes, tyres and rims.

- Tyre patch – an old plastic toothpaste tube is ideal.

- Pump. CO_2 canisters are a handy addition for that easy, fast fix but you will need a pump to deal with multiple flats or if your canister fails.

- Multi-tool and any specialist tools your bike may require.

- Replaceable dropout to fit your bike.

- Spare clothing and waterproofs for those bad weather days.

- Food, such as energy bars, chocolate, fruit. Think about how well it will travel over rough ground and pack enough to last the ride.

Make sure your helmet is the correct fit and the straps are done up properly.

>> SOME BASIC MOBILITY, STRETCHING AND STRENGTH EXERCISES

Shoulders are a part of the body that will suffer if we do not increase our strength and flexibility. A huge amount of the movement of the bike is driven from the arms and shoulders. They are the main centres that take all the load of your torso and hits from the trail. They are also subject to huge loads while scooping and lifting the bike. Shoulder injuries plague many riders and can cause huge discomfort in our everyday life. The exercises below were shown to me after a mega crash left me with the early signs of a frozen shoulder. I now repeat them on a daily basis to keep in shape to ride hard.

EXERCISE 1

Stand side-on to a wall or solid object as shown in the picture, with your upper arm relaxed at the side of your body and your forearm extended out in front at a 90-degree angle to the upper arm. Your palm should be facing inwards. Place the back of your hand against the wall and position yourself so you are parallel to the wall.

- Apply pressure outwards, slowly increasing the pressure while counting to nine.

- Relax and repeat the process with the other arm.

EXERCISE 2

Stand with your back to a solid object, preferably a wall. If possible get your heels in against the wall. With your upper arm relaxed against the side of your body, raise your forearm to 90 degrees, palm facing inwards and fingertips pointing ahead.

- Apply pressure with your elbow backwards, slowly increasing the pressure while counting to nine.

- You will feel your toes curl and dig in to the floor as the pressure is increased.

- Relax and repeat the process with the other arm.

EXERCISE 3

Stand facing the wall, with your upper arm relaxed next to your torso, and your forearm extended from the elbow at 90 degrees. Position yourself so that your closed fist contacts the wall and you are thus standing square to the wall.

- Apply pressure forwards, driving your fist through the wall slowly, increasing the pressure while counting to nine.

- Your heels will dig into the floor as you increase the pressure.

- Relax and repeat the process with the other arm.

EXERCISE 4

Stand square and upright, yet relaxed. Focus on a spot in front of you. With your palm facing backwards, lift your right arm up, behind your back, and aim for the centre of your shoulder blades. Simultaneously lift your left arm up and over, behind your head, with your palm facing inwards.

- Interlock your hands. If unable to do so, dangle something like a towel or old inner tube from your upper hand. Hold the material and gently stretch by lifting your upper arm.

- Repeat the exercise, switching the upper and lower arm/hand from right to left.

EXERCISE 5

Stand with your right arm out in front of you, raised up, palm facing upwards at shoulder height.

- Bring your elbow in, keeping your palm facing upwards so your hand rotates under your armpit.

- Keep extending rearwards, rotating the shoulder joint and wrist.

- Bring your arm forwards in a circular motion, with your palm still facing upwards. Twist the wrist to return to the start position.

- If you have a shoulder injury or cannot make full circles, start with the opening movement, repeating by tracing back the path your hand has taken, slowly increasing the motion rearwards and up on each session.

- Repeat the exercise several times, then switch and repeat using your left arm.

Ankles, knee and hip joints will also require attention as they too suffer from high-frequency bumps and dynamic manoeuvres.

EXERCISE 6

With your hands on your hips, place your foot out in front of you and slightly to the outside.

- With your toes pointed down and touching the floor, rotate the ankle gently in a clockwise motion, pivoting from the big toe.

- Repeat nine times then rotate the ankle in the opposite direction.

Exercise 6.1

- After nine revolutions of the above, raise the foot in the air and rotate your lower leg from the knee joint, keeping your foot in line with your shin and your toes pointing down.

- Repeat for nine revolutions.

- Gently slow to a stop and repeat the motion in the reverse direction.

Exercise 6.2

- When you have completed your ninth revolution from the knee in exercise 6.1, continue rotating in the same direction but now move your whole leg from the hip for another nine rotations.

- Slow the leg, having completed your ninth revolution, and repeat the process in the opposite direction.

EXERCISE 7

- Repeat exercises 6, 6.1 and 6.2 with the opposite leg.

Core strength is crucial, and by doing some extra work in this key area we decrease the likelihood of injury and dysfunction. Your abdominal muscles are a defence mechanism for your back, particularly the lower back. Ever had lower back pain? This could be caused by a bad riding position or cockpit setup, or a general weakness signalling the need to work on your core strength. Here are some exercises that can be done daily. Remember to work within your limits and take your time. Start small and work big.

EXERCISE 8

Stand in your neutral stance, with your arms at your sides. You should have your palms facing inwards to your thighs.

- Lean to your left, sliding your hand down the outside of your thigh. Stay focused, looking straight ahead, and resist the temptation to lean your head forwards.

- Return to the centre and repeat the movement on the opposite side. Your neck may bend slightly in the direction of the movement.

- Repeat daily, with approximately 20 repetitions to each side.

EXERCISE 9

Stand in your neutral stance, with your arms bent and raised to chest height. Place your hands together so that your palms touch. Your fingers should point to the sky. Feel the pressure through the wrists.

- Move your fingers from left to right, keeping your palms together.

- Repeat daily, with approximately 20 repetitions each side.

◎ **TIP**

Build flexibility over strength – inevitably we will build strength in the process.

EXERCISE 10

Stand in your neutral stance, raise your arms up to chest height and clasp your hands together.

- Rotate your wrists round in a smooth path in an anticlockwise direction. Remember to focus on a spot out in front of you.

- Rotate through a clean 360 degrees several times.

- Repeat the process in the opposite direction.

EXERCISE 11

Lie on your back, with your knees raised up and your legs together.

- Rock side to side, rotating at the hips.

- Do not overstretch and keep the motion smooth and fluid, like a metronome.

- Repeat a few times at first and increase the number of repetitions over time.

EXERCISE 12

Lie on your back, with your legs stretched out. Keep your legs together. Place your arms out to the sides at 45 degrees, palms facing the floor.

- Raise your legs together so your heels are about four inches off the floor.

- Hold for five seconds, raise the legs a further four inches and hold for five seconds.

- Keep your legs straight and move your legs apart. Do not fully do the splits just yet – pause at about halfway. Hold for five seconds.

- Now move your legs further apart so you are doing the splits and hold for five seconds.

- Reverse the process and hold at each stage on the return for five seconds.

◎ NOTE

This is a very tough exercise to perform – do not overdo it. Start with small movements and at first maybe only pause for one second each time. Build up each session and, as you get stronger, increase the duration of the hold.

EXERCISE 13

This exercise stretches the hamstrings and strengthens the lower back while working the lower abdominal region. Sit on the floor, with your back upright. Stretch your legs out in front, with your feet together. Keep your legs flat on the ground. Pull an old inner tube around your feet, gripping it at each end with the hands (you can use a scarf or similar if you don't have an old tube to hand).

- Pull yourself up and forwards, aiming to close the gap between your chest and thighs.

- Relax back into the tension on the inner tube and repeat.

- Repeat a few times to begin with, and increase the repetitions over time.

Sit-ups are also good abdominal fodder. I recommend you use an ab-crunch frame for sit-ups as it removes the pressure and load on the spine. It also helps keep you straight throughout the movement. To increase the workload, cross your legs when doing sit-ups. Remember to do them with your legs crossed in the opposite direction as well, to balance things out.

All exercise ranging from using free weights to a relaxing swim will benefit your riding in the long run. Even a walk in the hills will help keep you supple and strong. I highly recommend incorporating alternative training methods to complement your riding, but make sure you do not overstress the body, and seek professional assistance where necessary.

COMPETITION_

For some of you recreational riding is just not enough. Luckily there are a huge variety of competitions out there to suit your needs – from good old-fashioned cross-country races to the slightly more outrageous free-ride and slope-style events. As riders keep pushing the boundaries, event organisers keep conjuring up new formats to fuel their needs. Way back, as you will recall from Chapter 1, the Klunkerz from Marin county ran the Repack downhill. At a similar time, the guys rode their klunkers in a cyclo-cross race.

Cross country and downhill are the foundations of the sport – slalom, trials and uphill were introduced in the first non UCI accredited World Championships. In the years to come, riders could also compete in long-distance endurance events like the Idita Rod. This insane point-to-point race follows the famous dog-sled track through Alaska, a gruelling challenge that few complete. Events like the Kamikaze Downhill held on Mammoth Mountain in the US gave birth to legends as top riders from all over the world descended the mountain access road, hitting speeds in excess of 60mph. The nineties would see the introduction of marathon downhill, four-cross (4X) and 24-hour cross country.

Purpose built trails offer a consistent platform to measure your performance.

◎ TIP

For all disciplines you will need to develop your core techniques.

- Braking (*see* page 130)
- Neutral stance (*see* page 136)
- Shifting gear (*see* page 139)
- Looking (*see* page 149)
- Cornering (*see* page 151)
- Pumping (*see* page 171)
- Manuals (*see* page 173)

◎ COMPETITION PREPARATION

Mental preparation for a race in any discipline will be a factor to consider. A calm mind is required to focus on the task, and pre-race preparation can help eliminate race-day nerves. Get to know yourself and how you best deal with the situation. Some riders can turn up at the last minute with a dirty bike and just jump on and deliver, while others need days to prepare and have a more meticulous approach. Remember, there is no right or wrong way here and you may surprise yourself at just what works best for you.

I tried every possible way over several seasons just to see what works best for me, from a Formula One style polished approach to the last-minute prep and hassle-free style. One thing I do know is that I have confidence in the fact that I have prepared for the event, with all systems checked and time to breathe before things commence. For me organisation is key – it takes the stress factor out and my mind is clear and able to focus on the task in hand.

So the training is done, the van is packed and you're on your way to the competition. When you arrive sign in and, if you have not yet done so, check the timetable and plan your days. Walking the course before, during or after practice is highly recommended. There will be lines available that you may miss if you ride all day without taking time to look for them. Following known faster riders is another good way to discover those hidden lines – it will also improve your pace and give you confidence.

Adverse weather needs a slightly different approach. You will become a master of soil types and have to select different tyres for different conditions. All racers become educated in meteorology – watching the weather and practising the course as it changes to give them a feel of what it will be like come race time. Your training schedule should include practice on a variety of surfaces and in a multitude of different weather conditions.

Before you do any form of exercise, you should first warm up and stretch your muscles. I cannot emphasise enough just how important this is. It is also equally important to warm down and once again stretch those muscles out having completed a training session or ride. Riding mountain bikes using good technique requires you to move in a very dynamic fashion. You will also have to suspend your mass on your legs and arms, transferring huge loads through them and into the torso.

Stretching will radically improve your riding and recovery times. This in turn will allow you to ride harder, further and more often. In the process you will also be able to respond faster and therefore ride smoother. You will find various books out there covering different ways of stretching. The internet is also another great place to find out useful information on the subject. Be sensible and do not ride with an injury that could either get worse from the rigours of riding or affect your ability to ride in a safe manner.

Then there is the bike setup – tyre choice, as in other disciplines, can make or break a run. The constant compromise between traction and rolling resistance plays on everyone's mind. With physically demanding sections, gear ratios are another key component to get right. Too large a gear and the climbs will burn excessive calories and essential energy; too small a gear and you will be left behind on the open fast sections. These are just a few things to consider when entering a race. I highly recommend seeking some assistance from a regular competitor – they can offer advice on bike setup and preparation for the event.

Selecting the right tyre can be a bewildering experience for a novice.

PREPARATION KEY POINTS

You:

- Mental preparation
- Apparel
- Course riding/walking
- Warm up/warm down

Your bike:

- Condition
- Tyre selection
- Suspension settings
- Gear ratios

The event:

- Weather outlook
- Location
- Timetable
- Facilities/layout

>> CROSS COUNTRY

Cross country racing is a great way to improve your fitness and stamina. Drink lots of fluid and eat well to help with those workouts.

With the sport being driven by a group of athletes who were inspired by their mini wilderness adventures, early cross-country events had an epic vibe to them. The first world championships course was a staggering 32 miles long. Today race course lengths have shrunk and the professionals battle it out over much shorter race distances. The terrain has also changed, and the bike setup accordingly. Courses on the whole have become more sanitised than in the early years. This may be due to the introduction of endurance events or, on the other hand, it could be a result of race organisers adopting easier course designs to suit the ability of the mass market. No one can say for sure but, from my experience, it's rare to find a short-course cross-country competition that is technically challenging. When you do, revel in it – they don't come round that often.

Like all things, trends come and go. Racing cross country is no different and start-grid numbers have thrived and declined over the years. A boost to the start-grid economy came in 1996, when cross country finally made it into the Olympics in Atlanta. The media coverage and global credibility of such a prestigious event was a welcome lift to the discipline. Top riders from the road and even BMX were crossing over, seeking precious medals to match their rainbow stripes won in the World Championships.

Modern cross-country racing is easy to get into. There are many events that cater for this type of racing and the governing body, the UCI, has allocated a category system that allows novice riders to take part. You will have to train hard and earn points before you can progress to the next category. Age will also play a part in the selection of the correct category.

The bikes have changed little in appearance from early hard-tails but look closely and you will see many small details that have been polished and perfected. Full-on cross-country race bikes weigh as little as 8.5kg (19 pounds), their angles are tight and the ride is swift and nimble. As the technicality of the terrain increases, riders have to work harder to smooth out the trail. Racers will often save energy and avoid potential injury by running sections. Most of them have the skill set to do so, but favour longevity over whooping crowds.

To be a successful cross-country racer you will have to dedicate a serious amount of time to developing a large engine that can work hard. Training is a key component in winning races. Top racers take to the road to build a big base of pedal power and often compete in cyclo-cross events during the off season to keep their handling skills up to speed. As your fitness improves so does your ability to move through the terrain at speed, so

Simple smooth engineering, cross country bikes have a clean look to them.

you must never neglect your bike handling skills if you want to succeed in cross-country racing. That's not to say race organisers will throw you down a hill with monster north-shore gaps, but if you're prepared and can react accordingly there should be nothing out there that can't be ridden safely. A balanced training plan is the key to achieving great things on the circuit.

You will find that nearly all disciplines will require you to have a good base fitness. Strong muscular and cardiovascular systems are necessary to be successful, and riding a cross-country bike is a sure way to build these elements. Nearly all top athletes will train on cross-country bikes, building their skill level while gaining all-important overall fitness. It is the foundation of the sport and an important part of your training agenda.

◎ CROSS-COUNTRY TRAINING TIPS

The training focus here is on pedalling – long rides both on and off road are essential components. A coach will be able to measure your performance using various training aids and advise on the necessary workload accordingly. For a beginner this is not essential but, as you progress and your desire for podium positions increases, a coach will be able to give you that extra edge over your rivals. I have used a coach to increase my sustained power output and his advice has really paid off.

Start by creating a variety of rides that you can do consistently. This will give you a scientific-style base measure. This way you have a benchmark to work with and measure your performance against. Just ask yourself the question when you have finished a ride: 'How did I feel today?' It's a good idea to keep a journal or diary with notes on your ride and performance so you can see the improvements. You should:

- Make some of the rides similar in distance to your race events and others at least twice as long.

- Time the loop and make a mental note of the gears you are pushing at relevant points.

- Ride within your ability and make the session count.

- Try to get out and mix up your riding. Road riding will be hugely beneficial and makes for great winter training when trails are either snow-covered or too muddy to ride.

Sprint training, or interval training as it's sometimes known, is a great way to complement the large base fitness built up by riding mile after mile. The duration of your session will inevitably depend on your fitness level. You are advised to:

- Find a gradual uphill stretch in a safe location.

- Do a test run for your first sprint to gauge the length of time you can sustain a good quality pace.

- Start from a track stand or have someone hold you up.

- Sprint until the pace slows – you must give it all you have and be honest about when it's hurting and the quality is deteriorating. Aim for around five to ten seconds. You will have to repeat this process multiple times so please be realistic.

- Roll back down to your start point after your first sprint and wait five minutes. Repeat the process until the quality deteriorates. You will be doing well if you can give it 110 per cent for five repetitions. Please be aware that the side effects from sprint training can be quite nasty. You will quite possibly feel light-headed and dizzy and maybe even nauseous. I remember my first training session doing intervals – I threw up and could barely make it home.

Skills training will assist with your new-found speed and there are lots of things to practise as discussed in Chapter 6. The basic core skill drills will be most effective come race day. Also consider:

- Simple skills like fixing a puncture fast and mounting/dismounting your bike will also help in cross-country race events. Just think of all the little bits of time you save – it all adds up. There are so many places you can conserve energy by riding smooth and, in the process, shave off valuable seconds. With races being so tightly contested, these time savings could even make the difference between standing on the box or not.

- All areas of training should be given your best effort. If the quality dramatically deteriorates during the session then cut it short. Overtraining is a major problem and recognising the signs and getting to know the symptoms will increase your longevity in the sport.

- A performance coach will be able to write a specific programme to suit you and the type of event you are competing in. They do come at a cost but can give you in-depth advice, monitor your performance and possibly prevent you from doing too much or too little.

Prepare and practise for all conditions, a dry dusty day can turn into a mudfest overnight. Here a rider suffers the exact opposite as a soaked race course dries out.

- Track stand (*see* page 140)
- Wheelie (*see* page 166)
- Bunny hop (*see* page 175)

>> UPHILL KEY POINTS

RECOMMENDED SPARES

- Tyres
- Chains
- Chainrings
- Chainring bolts
- Cassettes
- Front and rear derailleur

>> TRIALS

The trials competition was another discipline those early riders who sought the rainbow jersey would have to deal with. Specific sections of trail would be marked out and riders had to clear the section without putting a foot down or, worst still, falling off. This type of competition had existed for years on motorcycles – mountain biking followed suit, with separate categories for both stock production bikes and specific, radically designed, trials bikes. The custom bikes use smaller wheels and lower, longer frames and run single-gear setups with a small chainring at the front.

Hopping is a key skill (see page 175) and course sections often require the ability to hop up onto and over large logs and boulders. There is room for multiple line choices as riders negotiate each section of the course, passing through gates marked within it. A score card is carried by the rider, and observers monitor their progress through the section. Penalty points are awarded, for putting a foot down for instance. The idea is to obtain no penalty points, or as few as possible.

Trials have never stopped growing in popularity, and you can often see riders performing demonstrations at shows and race events. The trials competition is a fantastic format. It brings the spectators close to the action, and demonstrates just how versatile the mountain bike is. The complexity of the courses has pushed riders' abilities to new heights. It is awe-inspiring to watch them leap from great heights and land with pinpoint accuracy in confined spaces and on narrow features.

To become a top trials rider you will have to spend many hours repeating manoeuvres on a wide variety of obstacles. Practice spots are abundant and the use of street furniture has been instrumental in creating modern-day street/urban riding. Hours of hopping around, learning how to pivot on either wheel and lurch forwards on the back wheel, are key. Like all the other genres, a level of fitness will develop from your hours and hours of riding, but to get ahead of the competition you will have to complement your riding with cross training. Climbing, martial arts, parkour and gymnastics will all help with your hand-to-eye coordination and flexibility. Your body will need to have the ability to move dynamically and absorb large impacts as you drop from great heights. Agility is the key, and this will come from core strength and flexibility.

Trials bikes are limited in their range, thanks to the small gear ratio and lack of a seat, but even a flat piece of ground can be turned into a complex section given a little imagination.

Most events will be run under UCI (the governing body in cycling) guidelines, so you will find a category system and easier stages for novice riders. Most top athletes in any sport start young, and the ability to bounce back when things don't go according to plan will be highly beneficial if you want to progress and become a top trials rider. Remember to practise in a safe environment and be responsible.

Some clubs will have members who ride trials but there are plenty of ways to meet people who share your enthusiasm. Get yourself to a competition and talk to the folk there – they will offer you advice on equipment and be able to tell you about other events and places to ride.

Not for the faint-hearted, trials turn an everyday architectural feature into a practice spot.

◎ TRIALS TRAINING TIPS

The phrase 'There is no substitute for time on the bike' really has a huge meaning for any aspiring trials rider. There is no need for long rides or those wretched interval sessions – just good old hopping around will do the trick. That's not to say they won't benefit you, as all riding is good riding, but there is not the emphasis on such training techniques as with other forms of mountain biking. Practise manoeuvres – including the essential rotations and lurching, on top of the above-mentioned cross training – and you're halfway to being world champion.

For those of you who have not ridden trials before, first master the necessary skills on the flat, then up and down curbs, before working on stairs and moving on to larger stand-alone drops and gaps. You will find a list of the key skills below, which are described in detail in Chapter 6.

>> TRIALS KEY POINTS

RECOMMENDED SPARES

- Brakes
- Brake pads
- Brake fluid
- Chainrings/retention device – bash guard
- Tyres
- Chains
- Chainring bolts
- Cranks
- Bars
- Forks/fork spares

>> DOWNHILL

The granddaddy, gravity-driven discipline has come a long way since Repack. Fully rigid bikes have been replaced by technological marvels that resemble fighter jets and race cars. Modern downhill bikes have huge, oversized suspension units to deal with the ever-increasing severity of the terrain. Course times have been capped for short-course racing but seemingly the distance remains similar to the early days. Courses now follow steeper fall lines and cross more severe surfaces. There was a trend in the nineties to use fast open-piste and forest road sections, where riders hit speeds in excess of 50mph. The average speed may have dropped but so has the use of four-inch-travel bikes. Only a few race tracks permit such high speeds on the circuit these days. That's not to say you will find it easy to reach those speeds even on those courses, as now courses often traverse such severe ground that you will have to train hard to stay on the bike and take the hits.

Point-to-point racing on your own against the clock requires a certain amount of mental preparation. Training the mind so it can block out all thoughts and simply process data from visual input and feeling is a key skill. Having the ability to make the right shapes at the right time to take out energy from the terrain, while simultaneously moving the mass of your body and vehicle through time, is the ultimate key to this type of racing. Riders have to pedal less, as the increasing gradient changes the skill set from hard pedalling and top technique to a battle in the mind – a battle every rider faces. Staying off the brakes is an obvious point to make if you want to ride faster, but in downhill racing the clock is the bearer of truth and its easy to talk about staying off the brakes, but harder to do it in practice while racing. The key to stringing together a flawless run is *focus* – you will need to have a lot of confidence, both in yourself and in

your equipment, to hit the right lines, stay off the brakes and pedal where you can.

I should point out that, although the top riders come across as relaxed, party people, make no mistake, they are top athletes too. There is a huge amount of endurance required to compete at the top end in downhill racing. You will have to go through many practice runs before and during competitions. Some riders train hard in the gym, but once again there is no substitute for time on the bike. Many of them ride motocross in the winter months to keep their eye in at speed and maintain the feeling of drifting and hitting large bumps. Your body will get beaten up pretty badly during a descent as you try to hold your mass up above the bike while it takes hits from below. The added effort of supporting yourself up against the braking force created from monster discs and efficient lever/calliper designs will mean tendon strength is equally important. Training should focus on the development of all areas of the body – but specifically the hands, wrists, arms and shoulders (*see* page 50 for exercise techniques).

Race events are plentiful, and again the relevant governing body will provide all the information required on what you need to compete in an event (*see* Appendix page 200 for more information). You will find the same

You will see some awesome sights when you hit big downhill runs. Here the author enjoys the sunset over Mont Blanc in the French Alps.

category structure as in cross country, but most downhill race tracks can be a bit more intimidating to a novice rider. You may want to use an uplift service or chairlift to pre-ride one of the many race courses out there to see if it is appealing enough before you hand over your hard-earned cash for a race licence and entry fee. I think it's fantastic that all over the world there are tracks cut for the purpose of racing, yet they are still open to the public to enjoy between events.

Personally speaking, I feel this type of racing is less cost efficient compared to the other options. There is a personal decision to make, which involves weighing how much your riding/racing costs against the amount of time you actually spend on the bike. If the result is evenly balanced, for some the scales are tipped by how much fun there is to be had rocketing downhill on one of today's amazing machines.

◎ DOWNHILL TRAINING TIPS

Top racers will train hard both in the gym and on the bike, hitting large off-road hills as well. Sprint training is very beneficial, and cross training is imperative if you want to mix it up with the best. You must develop all parts of your body with equal measure, working every muscle and tendon. Core strength is essential here as the body will be required to respond to trail input through sequences of dynamic moves. Some of the unpredictable situations you will end up in while racing downhill can be recovered if you are strong and supple.

To complement your riding, work on building tendon strength and muscle mass in the gym. This in turn must be supplemented by training your mind. It's no use if your body can take the hits but your mind can't deal with the processing of information. Enrol in a Pilates or Tai Chi class to help calm the mind while also increasing your core strength.

Cornering, pumping and jumping practice will be hugely beneficial in downhill racing. Work on your weaknesses and develop the key skills required to rocket down mountainsides. Once again, the core skills and specific skills sections in Chapter 6 will help improve your overall performance. A balanced training schedule is paramount in the trail to success.

>> DOWNHILL KEY POINTS

RECOMMENDED SPARES

- Brakes
- Brake pads
- Brake fluid
- Tyres
- Chains
- Chainrings
- Chainring bolts

- Cassettes
- Rear derailleur
- Cranks
- Bars
- Shifters
- Forks/fork spares
- Rear shock absorber/shock absorber spares

◎ SPECIFIC SKILLS REQUIRED

- Corners (*see* page 151)
- Drops (*see* page 180)
- Pumping (*see* page 171)
- Jumps (*see* page 184)
- Braking (*see* page 130)
- Manuals (*see* page 173)

>> DUAL SLALOM

The early gravity disciplines took their inspiration from skiing. Dual slalom competitions were hugely popular with both riders and spectators until the mid-90s. Some competitions still incorporate the discipline, although the style of track is slightly different from the early nineties dual slalom explosion.

The concept and course design was simple – two parallel runs down an average gradient were marked out with staggered blue and red gates of the type used for super giant slalom racing on skis. The course construction incorporated small jumps and bermed corners. In pairs, riders would run on each lane against the clock to qualify. The 32 fastest would be entered into the final elimination run-off. The fastest rider would ride against the slowest and the elimination process left four competitors to shoot it out for the podium.

BMX riders crossed over as sponsorship deals became lucrative. The close racing and compact course area is perfect for media coverage – add into the mix the odd inevitable crash and it's a dream format for manufacturers to gain exposure. Riders initially used their stock mountain bikes, and some even experimented by racing BMX cruiser bikes. These bikes jumped better, but the narrow 24-inch wheels were not as capable on the rough, loose ground. As stock bikes changed, riders adopted the more compact frames and eventually short-travel suspension.

Sometime around the mid-nineties, an event organiser came up with the genius idea of putting four riders together, but on a shared track. The fever spread and all over the globe race weekends adopted the new format. The familiar jumps and bermed corners were kept in to add a touch of spice to the racing. I remember competing in the first event of this nature in the UK in 1995 at the Mountain Biking UK Mint Sauce festival in Brighton. (Mint Sauce is a sheep featured in a cartoon strip drawn by Jo Burt. Mint and

Banked turns replaced open flat corners in dual slalom racing.

friends have graced the pages of Britain's largest-selling mountain bike magazine, *Mountain Biking UK*, for over two decades.)

Dual slalom racing, like all disciplines, requires training to be competitive. You will need a fast snap out of the start gate and the ability to carry high speeds through loose turns. Jump practice is imperative if you want to be up with the best, fighting it out for a podium position. The skill of squashing out jumps and accelerating hard and fast will be rewarded in this prestigious event format.

Unfortunately, dual slalom events are not as common as they once were, with 4X becoming the preferred format. I've heard rumours of it making a comeback and I hope they come to fruition. Dual slalom is a wonderful way to improve your cornering capabilities and race your mates without wiping each other out. You can easily mark out a course and start hitting turns (rather than your friends) in no time.

◎ DUAL SLALOM TRAINING TIPS

The main emphasis of your training should be on cornering and sprinting – interval training is essential if you want to become a top dual slalom racer. Most modern race courses will also require you to be able to jump and pump features in order to be competitive. Some time spent down the local BMX track or jump spot will help you float through double jumps and pump out rhythm sections. Cornering practice should be mixed between riding open flat turns and railing bermed corners.

As always, tyre selection is a vital component and the large array of tread patterns offered by manufacturers will give you lots to think about. Try using different cuts and compounds on different surfaces before you get to the competition. Most courses are built from soil and are often hard-packed – the practice sessions on race weekends will give you a chance to try different variations.

>> DUAL SLALOM KEY POINTS

RECOMMENDED SPARES

- Brakes
- Brake pads
- Brake fluid
- Tyres
- Chains
- Chainrings
- Chainring bolts
- Cassettes
- Rear derailleur
- Cranks
- Bars
- Shifter
- Forks/fork spares
- Rear shock absorber/shock absorber spares

>> FOUR CROSS (4X)

The popularity of 4X continues to grow today, and the simplicity of the bikes and every kid's urge to jump just fuels the scene. The courses have progressed a whole load from my initial experiences and you will now find larger jumps, drops and banked corners on most 4X tracks. Race events use hydraulic start gates to ensure riders do not jump starts – another crossover from the BMX scene.

4X has also given birth to a new breed of course designer – the tracks really are a work of art. Huge, sculpted double jumps and rhythm sections are interwoven with miniature rock gardens, table tops and berms. To build a world-class track takes time and huge quantities of material. A designer will create their vision in modelling clay or in a sand pit before putting the diggers to work. Phil Saxena is one of the most renowned people in the game and is often involved in the construction of 4X tracks for world cup events.

The physical requirements needed to be a top 4X racer have seen top track sprinters cross over to knobby tyres. A hardy snap out of the gate and sustainable sprint are key components of your toolbox. Jumping and pumping skills will also be required, and visits to the BMX track will reward you in the long run on the results sheet. There are many competitions held all over the world, from small local level comps to world cup and world championships. Since it is a format that is sanctioned by the UCI, there is a category structure that opens up this type of racing to everyone.

◎ SPECIFIC SKILLS REQUIRED

- Corners (*see* page 151)
- Drops (*see* page 180)
- Pumping (*see* page 171)
- Jumps (*see* page 184)
- Braking (*see* page 130)
- Fast acceleration – interval training (*see* page 60)
- Manuals (*see* page 173)

However, choose your course carefully – some tracks feature larger than life features that intimidate even the top professionals.

◎ 4X TRAINING TIPS

4X requires similar skills to dual slalom and downhill racing. Getting a quick start and an early advantage on your competition is key. This will enable you to choose the optimum line ride defensively and control the race. By getting out in front at the start you will also have a mental advantage over your fellow competitors. You only have to watch 4X legend Brian Lopez for the proof. His killer gate skills put him out in front in a matter of pedal strokes.

Sprinting, jumping and pumping should be your main focus in training sessions, but do not forget to put in those cross-country and road rides to help build a bigger engine and sustain your efforts for multiple runs. To win a 4X competition you will have to endure the most amount of runs as the elimination process cuts the field down to a final four – this is where a good base fitness will pay off. Once again, top racers will cross train using the gym and road bike to complement hours on the track. Most racers will also compete in BMX competitions, as the skill set is almost identical to 4X.

>> 4X KEY POINTS

RECOMMENDED SPARES

- Brakes
- Brake pads
- Brake fluid
- Tyres
- Chains
- Chainrings
- Chainring bolts
- Cassettes
- Rear derailleur
- Cranks
- Bars
- Forks/fork spares
- Rear shock absorber/shock absorber spares

Practising pumping and jumping will help with your race times.

◎ SPECIFIC SKILLS REQUIRED

- Corners (*see* page 151)
- Drops (*see* page 180)
- Pumping (*see* page 171)
- Jumps (*see* page 184)
- Braking (*see* page 130)
- Fast acceleration – gate practice (*see* page 60)
- Manuals (*see* page 173)

>> MARATHON DOWNHILL

If being beaten up by Mother Earth while descending mountainsides against the clock isn't enough, then thankfully you can enjoy the added pleasure of doing it over an epic distance with a bunch of other lunatics at your side. The introduction of endurance, mass-start downhill racing was another development of the mid-nineties. The now-infamous Mega Avalanche at Alpe d'Huez in France was the creation of George Edwards, director of UCC and a mountain bike racer from the early days. His vision was to create a style of racing separate from the UCI agenda.

The outcome was a point-to-point race that would test a rider's ability over 33km. The race starts at 3333m, at the top of Pic Blanc, and descends to the town of Allemont, some 2500m below. Riders line up, 25 per row, in a tight grid before shooting off down the piste and onto the glacier. Although the word downhill is in the title, to achieve such a distance, and to level the playing field between the technically proficient and the athletic riders, you will have to pedal along flat sections and up small climbs to reach the finish line. This is common in all types of marathon downhill racing, although different course designers will come up with different solutions to help even the field.

Psychosis was a hugely popular race in the US, run against the clock. One at a time, riders would depart from the start gate at timed intervals. The course also had uphill sections to test the riders' stamina, something George Edwards' Maxi Avalanche competitions also incorporate. These

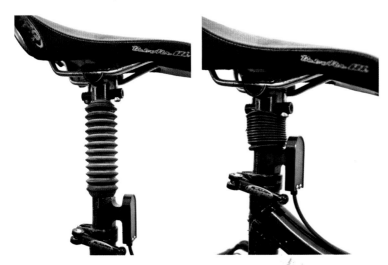

Having a seat post that drops by a remote lever on your handlebar can be a big advantage in marathon downhill events.

mini-versions of the Mega Avalanche event run a similar format to their big brother, but over a shorter distance. This means riders have to compete in two race runs to be crowned champion. We are now seeing many more twists on the format, and kitsch events, like the Red Bull Trail Fox, continue to change the way we need to train and prepare for events. I am a huge advocate of marathon downhill – at the turn of the century I made it my priority to seek out and master the ever-expanding marathon downhill scene.

There are so many elements to this type of racing, creating a never-ending list of options and possibilities. To be at the top of the game you have to be physically fit like a cross-country racer, strong like a downhill racer and super smooth like a top 4X racer. Your awareness has to broaden from short-course downhill racing as you deal with other riders around you – it really is an assault on the senses. Your peripheral vision tracks riders on all sides while you focus on trying to ride that optimum line you practised all day yesterday. Inevitably, you will have to dynamically change your line choice as the riders in front and around you move rocks about and block your favoured piece of earth.

Every organising crew and venue will run their own variation of the endurance downhill. There is no single governing body to sanction this type of racing and the UCI have shown no interest in affiliating with endurance events. Here in the UK a new organisation, B1KE, is establishing standards in gravity-assisted endurance racing. They have set out to raise the bar and run events with structured category systems that include controlled categories for specific tyre or bike manufacturers. The crew behind these events worked in partnership with George Edwards from UCC to bring enduro (see page 84) to the UK in 2007.

◎ MARATHON DOWNHILL TRAINING TIPS

Stamina and aerobic fitness will need to be complemented by nerves of steel to compete at the top level in marathon downhill. Riders battle it out over long distances, taking on technical terrain in the process. A fast start to get a clear trail is essential, although this huge effort will hinder you if you have not built a large engine, as you will need to sustain a high output for some distance to go. To add to the physical load, your brain will be deprived of oxygen, as nearly all marathon downhill events start at high altitude. Your nerves will be tested to the limit as you battle it out over thirty-odd kilometres against other riders. To win a prestigious event like the Mega Avalanche you will need the skills of a top world cup downhill racer and the fitness of a top world cup cross-country racer.

Folding tyres may travel well, but the sidewalls are thinner and may puncture easily.

Preparation for these events is essential. Only the foolhardy turn up and have a go without first having put in some big miles and experienced technical terrain. Long-distance cross-country and road rides will build a strong base but you must balance your training sessions with sprint

No looking back now.

Train hard, practise your skills and take that trophy home.

The winner of the 2009 Avalanche Trophy, Mike Thickens, relaxes before his race run.

training and cross training. Every part of your body will be worked over throughout a race run and the huge workload will be additional to the days of practice in learning the course. There are flat and uphill sections that will require some hard pedalling and you will have to ride on a multitude of surfaces, from snow and ice to deep dust and bedrock. You and your equipment will be tested to the limit. Accidents are frequent, either due to fatigue or caused by your fellow competitors' eagerness to overtake. Pacing is something you will have to consider and the potential for broken components is very high indeed.

Throughout the duration of a competition, you will have lots of opportunities to practise the course. This is essential in all forms of mountain bike racing. Courses are marked, allowing creative line choice, and there will be plenty of options to choose from. Once again it can be advantageous to ride with faster riders and the more experienced racers. You will need to save some energy for your qualification race and optimise your chances of getting that all-important grid position.

Other things to consider in these types of event include nutrition and hydration – the large workload and thin air will require essential sustenance. Another factor is a composed, calm, focused mind, which will help make split-second decisions as you battle it out with the best. The ability to dynamically change your line choice and tough it out will be required at the front of the field as large rocks roll across in front of you and riders try to pass in the craziest of places.

>> MARATHON DOWNHILL KEY POINTS

RECOMMENDED SPARES

- Brakes
- Brake pads
- Brake fluid
- Tyres
- Chains
- Chainrings
- Chainring bolts
- Cassettes
- Rear derailleur
- Cranks
- Bars
- Shifters
- Forks/fork spares
- Rear shock absorber/shock absorber spares

⊚ SPECIFIC SKILLS REQUIRED

- Corners (*see* page 151)
- Drops (*see* page 180)
- Pumping (*see* page 171)
- Jumps (*see* page 184)
- Braking (*see* page 130)
- Fast acceleration (*see* page 60)
- Manuals (*see* page 173)

>> ENDURANCE RACING: 6-, 12-, AND 24-HOUR RACING BY ROB LEE

Rob Lee is one of the most successful 12- and 24-hour racers in the UK, and is the best authority on this subject. He won the 24 Hours of Adrenaline World Championships in his age group in 2005 and was the first UK rider to win a gold.

The origins of 12- and 24-hour mountain biking are to be found somewhere in the United States in the early nineties. Initially, the events were open to teams only, with many believing that participating solo in such a race would be beyond the capability of the human machine. The original solo 24-hour is disputed but perhaps the most famous story is that of ultra-endurance legend John Samstad, who, so the story goes, entered a 24-hour race as a team where each of the four members of the team had names that were all variations of his name. He was, of course, the only member in the team, and so set about racing the entire event by himself. Many see this as the birth of the solo category – others dispute the fact. Whatever the reality of the situation, it's very clear that this story alone has inspired an entire generation to take up solo 24-hour racing as a serious discipline.

The first 24-hour world championships (which were not sanctioned by the UCI) were held in 2001 and won by American pro Chris Eatough. He was to go on to become one of the top 24-hour soloists, and the guy to beat at the worlds. In total Eatough won no fewer than six 24-hour solo world titles and was eventually dethroned by Australian pro Craig Gordon in an epic battle that saw both racers requiring medical attention and necessitated a three-day hospital stay for Gordon to save his kidneys!

During the early part of the century, 24-hour racing became the growth area of the sport due to the open nature of the events. With categories for solo

The riders progress is logged each lap in professional 24 hour pits; riding for 24 hours will take its toll – hydration and nutrition are essential; there are some wonderful characters you will meet out on the trail and at race events.

racers and for teams of four or five pairs, the events can accommodate large numbers of entrants, all of differing abilities and fitness levels. Some use the event as a social with friends, a whole weekend away riding bikes and sharing experiences, while others base their whole competitive season around one event and fight it out for the glory. The best-known events are the 24 Hours of Adrenalin World Championships (usually in Canada), the 24 Hours of Moab (Utah, USA) and Mountain Mayhem (UK).

The usual format for a 24-hour race course is very similar to that of cross-country world cup racing. Often a lap of the course is longer (usually somewhere between eight and eleven miles) but the technical nature is very similar. UK race courses tend to be a bit more tame than those in the US; however, the world championship course is in a whole different league. The winner of any category is the rider (or team) that completes the greatest number of laps within the 24-hour period. Occasionally, races last for 25 hours – riders who get through the finish just before the 24 hours is up keep going to complete that extra lap.

Physical preparation for solo 24-hour racing is very similar to that for cross country, with perhaps a little more emphasis given to endurance over out-and-out speed. The most important difference between the disciplines is that solo 24-hour racers spend a lot more time toughening themselves up and working on the mental side of their game. Any weakness in the area of mental strength will ruin a solo attempt, regardless of the athlete's physical fitness level.

Solo 24-hour racing has created a resurgence in long-distance record attempts, and multi-day rides in the UK have helped boost such events in other places around the globe. This seems to be the most logical area for growth within the sport at this time, as trail riding and adventure riding are

The never-ending job of looking after your teammate's bike continues through the night.

at an all-time high globally and heavily focused on in aspirational marketing campaigns by blue-chip companies around the world.

>> FREE-RIDE AND SLOPE STYLE

The introduction of long-travel bikes for downhill racing created another new genre of riding and competition – riders like Josh Bender from the US started to push the boundaries riding large drops. At a similar time in the mid-90s, Canadians on the North Shore were constructing raised wooden trails to ride over wet ground and in areas where the earth was too severe to pass at ground level. Both forms fused together and slope style was born. This format combines the ability to take large drops and gaps with riders adding flair to their giant leaps, performing flips and rotations as they fly through the air. The scene still seems to be influenced, be it subconsciously, by skiing. Free-ride and slope style follow the same principles, but slope style is associated with bike parks at ski resorts, while free-ride uses lines out in the hills that are not built or constructed.

For the first time mountain biking had a competition format that was not based on time and position. Slope-style competitions are won on points given for the complexity, consistency and smoothness of a trick. Riders take turns to put runs in, down a course littered with various jumps and drops. This type of riding really is not for the faint-hearted. Modern free-riders will flip huge gaps and put 360-degree rotations into monster shore drops.

The new wave of slope style has created yet more stars over the years – even top world cup downhill racers cross over in an attempt to score points and win valuable prizes. The world of free-ride and slope style has also brought with it new fashions and trends that have filtered through to other areas of the sport. We are increasingly seeing riders hit cross-country bike parks who are armoured up to the hilt in technical garments that have been derived from slope style and downhill. New companies have been created off the back of the scene and bike manufacturers cash in once again on another demographic. Slope style typically appeals to a younger generation – the hard knocks you have to go through in order to progress may have something to do with this, or it could just simply be that older men and women feel out of place in tight jeans and a bone-dome cycle helmet down the local jump spot – I'll let you draw your own conclusions here! What I can say is that slope style is here to stay.

The format is very interactive and makes great viewing for spectators. Free-ride and slope style have cemented mountain biking's image with the general public as being a cool extreme sport. We can also thank the discipline for improving the quality of DVD production. The large impressive tricks look even more impressive when filmed using state of

Tinker Juarez counts the laps before taking victory at Mountain Mayhem.

Wall rides are popular features in free-ride comps.

the art technology and big budget production. The high-quality mountain bike movie is all thanks to companies wanting to show their riders going larger in more insane locations than their rivals.

Slope-style bikes are bullet proof in their design and build. Depending on the terrain and scale of obstacle, riders will opt for bikes with travel in the four to six inches range. A few brave folk will run hard-tail dirt jump bikes but only on the smaller, smoother courses. Oversize everything, including bars, hub and bottom bracket width – these are the choice components for riders. Downhill bikes are often used for the purpose, but are rare in competition use.

There are competitions out there that cater for novice riders, but the larger events are usually by invite only. The event format normally consists of qualification runs and final run-offs. As this style of competition is not sanctioned by the UCI, different event organisers will run their own category splits. You will have to work hard on your jumping skills and armour up for safe progression at your local spot. Riders will use trampolines and foam pits to master new tricks – repetition is the key here. The more times you repeat your manoeuvres, the deeper they become set in your subconscious. Muscle memory retained in the practice arena will respond according to task when the time comes to roll out to the start area at your first comp.

Local spots are a great place to meet enthusiasts and share knowledge. Bike shops in your area will know about local spots where riders meet and should be able to point you in the right direction. The scene exists on a network of trails that range right across the spectrum, from professionally built installations at specific bike parks to a huge network of counter-culture built non-official sites. The never-ending debate continues in rider circles and in the boardroom. The designers and land owners have design constraints that can only deliver so much – the problem is that riders' desires and abilities have far surpassed what the trails can deliver.

◎ SAFETY FIRST

When you find a spot make sure it is safe to ride and do the right thing by telling someone where you will be and when you intend to return. This type of riding is dangerous and riding spots can often be in remote locations. Do not ride structures that are not built to a high standard and ride within your limits. Start small and work big.

◎ SLOPE STYLE TRAINING TIPS

To progress in this discipline you will have to add some artistic flair to your standard jumps and drops. A lot can be learned from motocross and BMX, where riders have been pushing the boundaries for many years. To get noticed and pick up sponsors, riders have to dedicate hours and hours to the foam pit or lake jump. There are many ways to practise manoeuvres, including lying on your back with your bike above you. A trampoline may also be very beneficial but you will have to strip down an old frame and pad it up to use it safely. Practising slope-style riding isn't easy and you're guaranteed to take a few knocks along the way – be sensible and wear the appropriate protective clothing and this should help eliminate any unnecessary injury. However, there will come a time when you have to take to the dirt and timber trail to lay down your tricks.

Once you have mastered matching features by jumping, it's then time to add some artistic flair to your air time. You will also need to take your hands off the bars and kick your feet in various directions. The scene has a seemingly never-ending list of tricks that all boast creative names to accompany them – 'no footers', 'bar spins', 'can cans', 'supermans' and many more. The manoeuvres closely resemble those achieved by a gymnast, and the trampoline is a fantastic training tool that will help you master rotations. You do not need to put in huge miles and develop a large cross-country style engine, but once again a high level of fitness is required here to haul a 30-pound+ bike through the air.

Cross training will be beneficial as you will need to have strong muscles and tendons to deal with all the knocks and bumps. Being supple and flexible will also help in dealing with situations when you just get it wrong and eat dirt. Once again, Tai Chi and practices like yoga and Pilates will help build core strength and flexibility. Looking after your body is key to a long, fruitful career. Repeating tricks again and again will enable you to perform the most amazing feats consistently and effortlessly.

Watching DVDs and videos on the internet to see the detail of riders' actions while dropping gaps and jumping from quarter pipes will give you a greater understanding of how tricks are performed. Competing or training with better riders is a sure way to improve – they can give advice on how to pull tricks and will offer support and encouragement.

Your local skate park will have features similar to those found in a comp.

>> STREET RACING KEY POINTS

RECOMMENDED SPARES

- Brakes
- Brake pads
- Brake fluid
- Tyres
- Chains
- Chainrings
- Chainring bolts
- Cassettes
- Rear derailleur
- Cranks
- Bars
- Shifters
- Forks/fork spares
- Rear shock absorber/shock absorber spares

>> ENDURO

Enduro racing is a relatively new format for some riders, although I have heard rumours that the Norwegians have been racing in this way since the late nineties. Other parts of the world have created their own enduro formats, all of which differ slightly. The discipline is best described as being similar to that of a car rally. The course is made up of liaison, or link, stages that take riders on a mini wilderness adventure to compete individually against the clock in closed special stages. These special stage sections are predominantly downhill, but riders do have to use some physical effort as the stages will have flat and uphill sections. Stage length will vary depending on who is running the event; the number of times you ride the stages will also differ.

Enduro has spawned many new concepts in racing and they all have similarities that put them into this new category, or genre. Some race events will require team entries, while others may use a simpler format where riders race to the top for one special stage, then race down on a more technically challenging trail for the second and final stage. Yet again it's thanks to renegade outfits willing to push the boundaries that we have been blessed with this new style of racing. Like 24-hour racing the UCI have failed to adopt enduro, leaving little in the way of stringent guidelines and rules. This in turn allows event organisers to use their imagination to conjure up the many different event formats.

Riders are revelling in the new style of racing as they get maximum value for money from these types of event. It's all about riding, and you may find yourself in the saddle for up to six hours. Compare this to a few minutes in a downhill event and you can see why the racing is great value for money. Enduro also requires the use of a typical trail or all-mountain bike, making it slightly more affordable. There is no need to have a specific race bike and separate trail bike. The margin between chequebook champions, who usually benefit from state of the art equipment, and your everyday privateer has gone with enduro. The art really requires good all-round fitness and top-quality bike handling skills if you are to be on the podium.

You will find lots of events, often in beauty spots around the world – the internet and magazines are your best sources for finding them. Cycling is generally associated with being a community and online there are community-based websites that have user groups for all types of discipline. Certainly here in the UK the big buzz in the race scene is around enduro. Manufacturers have welcomed this relatively new form of racing with open arms, as it reaches the largest demographic of bike buyers and just continues to open up the sport, making it accessible to more people.

Charlie Williams from MTBSkills means business. Racers push the limits of physical endurance and technology.

Rider briefing is an essential part of your race weekend.

◎ ENDURO TRAINING TIPS

The discipline of enduro encompasses all types of riding. Its roots are cross-country based and liaison stages will require lots of pedalling where the key is to pace yourself and be efficient. The timed sections will test all your trail-riding skills and overall fitness. Long base rides and specific downhill training are going to be most beneficial if you want to progress through the ranks. See the previous sections on cross country and downhill for key training points (page 58 and page 66).

◎ SPECIFIC SKILLS REQUIRED

- Corners (*see* page 151)
- Drops (*see* page 180)
- Pumping (*see* page 171)
- Jumps (*see* page 184)
- Braking (*see* page 130)
- Fast acceleration (*see* page 60)
- Manuals (*see* page 173)

>> ENDURO KEY POINTS

RECOMMENDED SPARES

- Brakes
- Brake pads
- Brake fluid
- Tyres
- Chains
- Chainrings
- Chainring bolts
- Cassettes
- Rear derailleur
- Cranks
- Bars
- Shifters
- Forks/fork spares
- Rear shock absorber/shock absorber spares

>> KITSCH EVENTS

Over the years we have seen many competitions as either stand-alone events or demonstrations. The bunny hop comp was always a favourite of mine. A personal best of 38 inches at the legendary Malvern Hills Classic here in the UK, sometime around 1995, still has a special place in my heart. Crowds used to gather after a day's racing, and some goofing around inevitably turned into more testosterone-fuelled action as riders would try to outdo each other. I remember one year when the hop comp was reversed after the winner was announced and we competed in a limbo competition. You will still see hop demonstrations at bike shows and shopping malls, even today.

Lake leaping was another fringe event at the Malvern Hills Classic but this craze really was only for fun and it never took off. Nowadays free-riders will leap into water, practising manoeuvres for competitions. Long-jump competitions have also been held as fringe events and crowd-pleasing post-race shows. Mountain bike long jumping has taken on a whole new dimension, with riders being towed in by motorbikes and jumping insane distances. Pedal power just simply isn't enough for some people, but its rare now to see a long-jump competition.

The Kamikaze was one of the early stand-alone events that inspired folk to follow the new trend of mountain biking. Mammoth Mountain in California hosted this crazy test of speed, a point-to-point downhill race unlike any other. Riders hit insane speeds on the rudimentary technology of the time and accidents were commonplace. The race created stars and any rider featuring on the podium would rocket to stardom. The late, great Jason McRoy made his debut at the event in 1993, and images of him tearing up the course are still used today.

Red Bull hit the scene in the latter part of the nineties and stand-alone events became commonplace. One such event, the Gold Rush, involved riders descending into a disused mine and racing against the clock in an unusual mini-downhill. Who knows what new formats will be conjured up in the years to come.

EQUIPMENT_

As you will have discovered in the previous chapters, there are many styles of riding and a huge array of equipment to support them. Unfortunately it can be quite costly to equip yourself for certain disciplines, but buying good quality equipment will pay off in the long run. The cycling industry is one place where the saying 'You get what you pay for' rings true. Thankfully, though, there are reviews in magazines and helpful, smiley faces down your local bike shop to help you out. In this chapter you will find an overview of equipment and some useful suggestions on things to carry when out riding. Just remember to learn how to use the tools of the trade so you don't come unstuck out in the wilderness.

Before you can equip yourself with the correct clothing and protective wear you will have to choose the right bike for the job. When buying a bike take into consideration what you want it for. You may find that you need more than one bike to satisfy your riding needs. Luckily, nowadays there are five- and six-inch-travel all-mountain bikes that are capable of dealing with most types of terrain; however, these bikes will not perform as well as a bike designed to do a specific task. Larger-travel all-mountain bikes are not as fast or as light as thoroughbred cross-country race bikes but they will take on much larger terrain with ease. They are comparable to full-on downhill bikes but once again will not perform as well as one for extreme environments. There is inevitably a compromise to be made when buying an all-round bike.

When you are ready to part with your hard-earned cash, shop around to get the best deal. Bike models are often updated on an annual basis before the year is out, as manufacturers release next year's model earlier and earlier in the current year. You may be able to get a better deal on a bike that is about to be replaced by a new model. Most component parts have a generic fit to them so it's no problem if you get a bike that is equipped with last year's kit and then upgrade parts when you have worn them out. Try to avoid components that have been in production for less than 12 months, as quite often these parts will be upgraded and refined in a short space of time. The same goes for frames and forks. Waiting for second generation versions of things can be very advantageous, as all the teething problems should be resolved and the likelihood of you having any issues with them is greatly reduced.

>> WHICH BIKE SHOULD I CHOOSE?

>> CROSS-COUNTRY TRAIL AND RACE BIKES

These bikes are intended for all-out cross-country riding and racing. They are light in their build and will be very efficient for pedalling. They are built for covering ground fast and will be far more efficient than longer-travel suspension bikes. I highly recommend riding a hard-tail, as they force you to develop good technique in order to cover ground smoothly. Old-school riders who had no option are easy to spot from their technique – having spent years on hard-tail bikes they seem to float through trails using skill and finesse, rather than letting the bike plough through rough ground. Hard-tails are a great way to develop a large skill base which is highly beneficial when you progress to full-suspension bikes.

You will find frames made from all manner of materials, each offering different ride qualities; the longevity of the materials will also differ slightly. Most cross-country bikes are equipped with 27 gears, usually by Shimano or SRAM, and 26-inch wheels are the norm, although 29-inch wheels have grown in popularity over the last few years. The advantages of a 29-inch wheel are the increased stability and the ability to roll over rough terrain; the disadvantages are the lack of rim and tyre choices. At the cheaper end of the market, bikes typically come equipped with basic suspension forks. This is an area to research in greater depth when buying a bike, as the benefits of a fork that has adjustable compression, rebound, spring weight or air pressure will be useful in achieving better handling qualities and a smoother ride.

Steel bikes are a fantastic way to go, offering a slightly supple ride but without being too lazy in their response to pedal input. Steel frames can also be easily repaired should you damage them and, providing you do not expose the bare metal to the elements, they will last for years and years. These frames can also be reheat-treated to bring back that zippy responsive feeling which fades over time.

Aluminium frames are very common, and oversize tubes allow the manufacturers to reduce the wall thickness, producing very strong and lightweight frames. They are more often than not lighter than their steel cousins, making them first choice for many recreational and competitive riders. The downside to thin walls is the likelihood that they will be dented by flying rocks or if you crash, dropping the bike on rocks and stumps. Aluminium gives a very fast responsive ride but some people find it a little harsh and unforgiving. The material is also liable to work hardening and over time the frame will go off, losing its responsiveness, and the potential of cracking in key areas increases. It is also slightly harder to get paint to adhere to its surface and paint flaking can be an issue with aluminium frames. Nowadays most companies either anodise or ball burnish their frames to avoid this happening.

Titanium frames live in the rare and exotic category. The material is hard to machine and weld so frames come at a price. One main benefit of a titanium frame is the longevity – titanium's corrosion-free super-strong properties mean a frame fabricated out of it will outlast all others. Titanium bikes offer a plush ride as the material is capable of flexing ever so slightly, but this does not impede its performance, though – it enhances it. As you put power through the cranks they seem to store up that energy and convert it into forward motion. These bikes ride like no others and are worth every penny in my opinion. Look out for quality material from the likes of Sandvic when selecting a frame. There are some companies sourcing metal from other places but the ride quality (and the price) is noticeably lower than a frame fabricated from Sandvic tubing.

Carbon fibre is the ultimate luxury material used by top manufacturers, being incredibly strong and incredibly light when produced in the correct manner. Carbon frames are the Gucci of mountain bike design and build. Their ultra-light weight usually comes with a contrastingly heavyweight price tag. Once again these frames are susceptible to damage from both foreign objects and crashes, and the material also deteriorates with age and use. Thin strands of Kevlar are bonded together using various epoxy resins and this glue breaks down over time as the frame flexes. Even slight imperfections in the material can have dire consequences and crash damage can result in weakening the frame, if not destroying it. Many racers will save their bikes for race time only, favouring a different bike for training purposes.

Look for a reputable brand of tubing when buying a steel frame.

Large oversize tubes and hydro forming are commonplace on modern aluminium frames.

Titanium is hard to machine – the exquisite detailing on the Yeti ARC-Ti comes at a price.

Carbon fibre bikes are light, but heavy on the wallet.

>> SHORT-TRAVEL FULL-SUSPENSION: 80MM TO 120MM

Aimed at filling the void between all-mountain bikes and hard-tails, short-travel bikes and soft-tails are a fantastic compromise for those who want to be pedal efficient and yet not suffer from a harsh ride. Once again manufacturers will use a variety of materials to make strong, lightweight bikes and quite often you will get frames from mixed materials. These bikes are built for cross-country racing and trail riding and are more than capable of dealing with rough terrain. You will need to ride a little more tentatively in severe conditions, however, as the geometry is not dissimilar to a hard-tail. Steep angles keep these bikes feeling tight, nimble and responsive but can be slightly unnerving on steep gradients. The shock absorbing is provided through a small linkage system and lightweight air shock absorber. Most bikes have intelligent valving systems to eliminate movement from the rider's input through the pedals and are often adjustable on the fly, so the bike can be tuned to suit the current terrain. Once again look at the forks and consider spending just that little bit extra to get a good quality adjustable fork.

Steep tight geometry and a low weight are the basis for all short travel cross country bikes.

>> DIRT JUMP AND STREET BIKES

There are some real bargains to be had if you want a bike to ride down the local skate park or jump spot. The simplicity of the bikes means manufacturers can price them accordingly. They do not have to be as refined as trail and race bikes, so you will find the compact frames are noticeably heavier than their cross-country counterparts. Frames are usually made from steel, although some riders will opt for aluminium versions. Off-the-peg bikes have single-speed setups and short-travel forks, low riser bars and basic disc brakes. These bikes will come ready to roll on low, profiled knobby tyres sitting on super-tough aluminium rims. Built to last and to be thrown away on hard surfaces when you get it wrong, street and dirt jump bikes are pretty much indestructible.

Frames specifically for four-cross (4X) are out there, but in small numbers. Compact and race-ready lightweight builds come in short-travel full-suspension and hard-tail variations. The angles will vary depending on the manufacturer, but expect to see head angles in the 71-degree range and seat angles around the 68-degree area. Some companies produce slacker head angle frames to accommodate longer-travel forks – your local dealer should be able to advise what fork suits what frame.

Compact drive components and super stiff cranks take the knocks with ease.

>> TRIALS BIKES

For those of you wanting to hop around, trials bikes are the way forward, but they are specific to the task, so you will not be able to use them for any other purpose. Small-geared compact frames are typically fabricated from aluminium, usually lack a seat and come with 20-inch wheels that are fitted with monster, wide sticky tyres. Cheaper models will be equipped with rim or disc brakes that are operated by cables; the more expensive versions will boast fancy hydraulic rim brakes or disc brakes. Top models will also come equipped with a front-mounted freewheel to allow you to roll backwards keeping your cranks level – a trick feature that is essential at the upper end of competition use.

>> MEDIUM-TRAVEL/CROSS-COUNTRY AND ALL-MOUNTAIN: 120MM TO 160MM

The larger sector of the market and the all-rounder, medium-travel bikes are the jack of all trades. They are capable of whisking you around the mountains, dealing with long climbs thanks to intelligent pro pedal devices and clever linkage systems. Equally capable in rough technical terrain for both climbing and descending, these bikes are sure to give you great value for money. You will find a huge variety of bikes in this area of the market and there are lots of good bargains to be had. When buying any complete setup, take into consideration the hidden components that manufacturers equip them with in order to save money – you may be better off spending just a little bit extra in order to get some more robust equipment.

Ask your dealer about the type of bearings used in the hubs, headset and bottom bracket – the sealed cartridge type are much longer lasting and smoother running. You should also enquire about spares for the bike, including replaceable mech hanger, pivots, bushings and bearings. Usually the more complicated the linkage system, the more likely it is going to cost you to replace worn parts. Ask yourself if the advantages of smoother pedalling outweigh the ongoing maintenance costs.

Manufacturers will bamboozle you with complicated terminology in an effort to make their bike that little bit more desirable than the others out there. Your local retailer should be knowledgeable enough to translate this jargon into layman terms and advise on what bike would be best for you. Medium-travel bikes also come in a multitude of different materials but the most common of all is aluminium. Once again, the finishing will depend on the manufacturer and model, but you should consider this when making a purchase. Powder coat finishes are harder-wearing than paint and will be lighter – but only just. These bikes are the weapon of choice for all-day trail rides and enduro-style race events.

They ride light and climb well, they also take on the rough stuff with ease. All mountain bikes have grown in popularity thanks to their versatility.

>> LONG-TRAVEL/ALL-MOUNTAIN AND FREE-RIDE: 160MM TO 180MM

As the travel increases so does the weight. Bikes in this area of the market are built to deal with the most severe terrain, so oversize tubing, braze-ons for chain devices and, quite often now, bolt-on rear axles will be commonplace. These bikes are still capable of climbing and, compared to a full-on downhill bike, are very pedal efficient. However, they will require more effort than a shorter-travel bike to get you to the top of your favourite descent. You will reap the rewards for your hard work once you have reached the top as monster oversize forks and suspension units soak up the large bumps and holes. The bikes have slightly slacker geometry than their little brothers, but are still just that bit steeper up front, compared to a downhill bike. Head angles are around the 67-degree mark, compared to slightly steeper 70-degree angles on the smaller-travel bikes. Remember to look at bearing types in key areas and ask about replacement parts.

>> LONG-TRAVEL/DOWNHILL AND FREE-RIDE: 180MM+

The Mac Daddies of downhill racing and free-ride are built with one thing in mind – if it's pedalling you're after or street riding, then look elsewhere. You will be in for a large bill in this department whether you build a bike from scratch, by carefully choosing your own components, or simply get a ready-to-ride off-the-shelf setup. Huge money goes into R&D in this

area, as it does in all areas of the bike industry, but the lower production numbers and cutting-edge technology design add that little extra value to downhill bikes. Once again there are a multitude of different linkage systems to choose from and lots of reviews on the internet and in magazines to help you.

A good guide for you budding world cup racers is to see who's who in the game and what they are riding. Most people on the scene are friendly and approachable, so talk to other riders to get a broader perspective and honest opinion on the different bikes out there. Demo days and uplifts are a good place to borrow bikes and have a go to see how they feel, but don't forget that, by changing cockpit and shock absorber settings, the same bike could feel radically different on the same trail. Demo days are good to get a go, but you will be limited on time and spares. Just bear in mind that different rider styles suit different bikes, and making small adjustments to suspension and cockpit setup can radically change a bike's characteristics.

>> THINGS TO LOOK OUT FOR WHEN BUYING A COMPLETE BIKE

>> FRAME SIZE

I personally feel there is a popular misconception in buying guides when it comes to selecting the correct frame size. The old-school way of thinking is derived from the sizing process used when buying a road bike – mountain bikes are a world apart and the skill set for mountain biking differs enormously. Sure, it is critical to have enough stand-over height on the bike but the key dimensions on a mountain bike relate to the top-tube length and front-centre measurement, not the seat-tube height. Most bikes now come in small, medium and large but people still look to buy and sell on the seat-tube height. The critical thing is reach and wheelbase – a good bike shop will offer to change stems in order to get the bike to fit correctly. It is important to note that the reach should be adjusted by changing stem length and not by moving the saddle in the fore and aft directions. This latter adjustment is related to your knees and pedals/cranks, and not to the reach. You will find some handy hints on setting up your rider position in Chapter 6.

A shorter wheelbase bike will be more responsive and nimble but will be twitchy at higher speeds; a bike with a longer wheelbase is much more stable but less manoeuvrable. Make sure you are not knocking your knees on the bars or so stretched out that it's hard to lift the front wheel.

Different people like different qualities from their ride and trying a multitude of bikes and setups is the only guaranteed way to find the best solution for you. Concentrate on what feels right before making a commitment, and once you've got that sweet-feeling setup make a note of its geometry and use this as your base measure. I rode small frames for over fifteen years and changes in geometry and sizing mean I now ride medium bikes with very short stems. The short stem helps with direct steering and an easy leverage point in the front end, and the slightly longer wheelbase makes the bike more stable at speed.

>> GEOMETRY

I could go into great depth with detailed explanations here but the mysterious world of bicycle geometry would be a whole book in itself. There are no hard and fast rules as to what is the best geometry for a mountain bike. Different riders have different rider styles and, when it comes to full-suspension frames, making adjustments to air pressure and/ or spring weights will change the standard geometry of a frame that has been produced on a jig. The bicycle company Specialized use a simple guide that describes a bike as being nimble, neutral or stable. A nimble bike will be steeper in its angles than a neutral bike and, at the opposite end of the spectrum, a slack-angled bike will be described as stable.

Larger travel bikes have slacker angles making them more stable at high speed.

Try out different brands before you buy. Don't be fooled by the marketing department, find a product you like and stick to it.

So to keep things easy – test ride before you buy, try other people's bikes and trust in what feels right. Variety is the spice of life and the key to finding your own sacred geometry. To summarise:

• Nimble: Steep angle – cross country/race

• Neutral: Neutral angle – trail riding/all-mountain

• Stable: Slack angle – all-mountain/downhill

>> COMPONENTS

For various bike models, you will be offered different levels and ranges of equipment, all of which should be suitable and fit for purpose. Most bikes will have either Shimano or SRAM gear sets, with brakes from Shimano, Avid (SRAM corporation), Haze, Formula, Hope or Magura. These manufacturers are the most popular selection for bike companies but, although they are the main players at present, some companies will spec other brands. At the lower end of the market you will have cable-operated disc- or cantilever-style brakes but most mid-priced bikes will have state of the art hydraulic systems. Dirt jump and street bikes often have cable-operated systems due to the nature of the riding. It would be expensive and annoying to ruin a session at the skate park if every time you crashed your bike, the brake hoses split, pouring fluid everywhere and finishing your ride early. On complete bikes, as mentioned earlier, look closely at headsets, hubs and bottom brackets – usually you will find cheaper components in these key areas, compared to the other parts in the group set.

Wheel sets are another place where manufacturers will shave some quality in an effort to keep prices down, so don't be surprised if you have to rebuild and replace wheels in the not so distant future. Expensive wheel sets cost a lot for a very good reason – factory-built wheels are never as strong as hand-built or hand-finished ones. Get your dealer to re-tension your wheels at the first service, if necessary.

The advantages of higher-grade equipment will be marginal for everyday riders and you could save a bundle by getting a bike equipped with slightly cheaper components. They may be a little heavier and may not look quite so bling, but they will inevitably wear out. If your love of the sport has grown then this is the time to treat yourself to some fancy bike bling. By going for the cheaper option in the first place, you will also have had some time to save up and have first choice of the latest technology.

>> ACCESSORIES AND NECESSITIES

Now that you have a bike it's time to kit yourself out with the appropriate equipment. The demands and rigours of mountain biking require us to be well prepared, and it is essential to keep both your bike and your personal equipment in tip-top condition. Worn equipment can fail when you need it most, leaving you in dire straits. By using good quality kit and maintaining it, you will reduce the potential of failure.

>> HELMETS

A suitable helmet for the task is essential – a person who rides without the correct helmet, or with a helmet that is ill-fitting and in poor condition, is a very foolish one. I owe a lot to cycle helmets and have suffered many head impacts and traumas over the years, and I can truly say that, if it were not for using good quality equipment, I would not be able to pass on my advice to you. Although it may not be law in certain places, it is, however, common sense.

For you cross-country riders there are many open-faced well-vented helmets out there. Look for recognised brand names and the CE logo or the SNELL and ANSI logos for quality assurance and your country's compliance with regard to safety standards. All this information should be available at your local shop and certainly on the internet. Your governing body and country's federation will also have information on the latest tests and requirements.

Concrete and wooden structures are often less forgiving than natural ones, making skatepark and street riding just as dangerous as all-mountain riding. Once again you will find a range of approved helmets in your local specialist shop for these activities. These helmets are often built with more material than cross-country ones, as venting is less of an issue. Get your local shop to advise on the correct helmet for the job and help you with finding the correct fit.

Free-ride and downhill riders opt for full-face helmets, which are much more bulky and closely resemble motor racing helmets. I personally use a motocross helmet for downhill racing and riding – these pass a UK standard that includes tests for the strength of the chin-guard area. Some cycling-specific full-face helmets only comply with legislation in the cranial area and not the chin guard, but that's not to say they won't be an improvement in a face-plant scenario. It's just that there is no data available to determine the loads that this area of the helmet can withstand. This is currently a huge debate and riders are arguing that motocross helmets are designed to withstand much larger impacts and so are less effective at dealing with smaller ones.

Full face helmets are a must for downhill and free-riders. Make sure it is in good condition and meets the safety criteria.

My views are drawn from the fact that I have been in some huge face-plant and cranial crash scenarios and would rather err on the side of caution and cover myself in the event of another huge impact to one of the most vulnerable areas of my body. A small concussion for a smaller hit seems like a trivial matter compared to the chin guard holding out in a monster stack. Maybe the data will be available by the time this book goes to print – just make sure you buy and use a well-fitting reputable brand. After all, you do not want to put a price on your life.

>> EYE WEAR

Without eye protection, there is a risk of mud, water, insects and low branches coming into contact with your all-important eyeballs. Damage to an eye is bad enough, but at 30mph on a single track there is a whole lot more at stake. Good quality glasses, designed for riding, will have replacement polycarbonate lenses and grippy, rubber ear and nose pieces will keep them in place as you perspire. Yet again go for an established brand and back up good frames with an assortment of lenses for the varying light conditions. Clear lenses are great for night riding and dull days, but you will need tinted lenses for those summer days in the saddle.

You may want to use motocross goggles – if you're free-riding or descending in your full-face helmet, they will integrate with it and give optimum cover. When wearing goggles in adverse weather conditions, it is best to use tear-off lenses. These super-thin lenses can be applied over the existing ones – when they get covered in grime you simply grab the tab and tear them off, revealing fresh clean lenses underneath.

>> GLOVES

There are lots of options when it comes to choosing gloves, but getting a good fit is key. I highly recommend full-fingered gloves as these give you just that bit more protection. Make sure your fingers fit snugly, as excess material could impede your braking ability.

>> SHOES

Specific cycling shoes come in two distinct styles and will have either rigid soles for use with cleats, or soft soles for use with flat pedals. Many manufacturers produce shoes that resemble low-cut walking shoes. These are OK for leisure riding on easy trails, but if you start hitting rough terrain and need to move the bike around more, then look at 5:10 or

Shimano for shoes constructed with soft compound-rubber soles. Cross-country racers tend to opt for stiff soles, but downhill and trail riders seek out the brands that offer a more flexible sole on their clip-in shoes. There are a few manufacturers who produce specific shoes for trials riding and information about your local retailer can be found on the internet.

>> SHORTS/TIGHTS/PANTS

There are many different types of leg-wear available and you will benefit from owning a range of garments to deal with a multitude of different weather conditions. Cross-country riders will use Lycra shorts, similar to those worn by road racers when the weather allows; in cooler climates a pair of Lycra tights is preferred. A huge majority of cross-country trail riders will opt for a pair of baggy outer shorts, with either cycling shorts underneath or an internal liner for comfort and hygiene. Be careful not to wear shorts that are too baggy and could catch on the bike or in a wheel.

Long waterproof leggings or outer shell trousers are a fantastic choice for rides in the depths of winter, and another great option for shorter, more intense, rides are waterproof shorts. They do come with a hefty price tag, but they have revolutionised winter riding. Downhill and free-riders choose either baggy outer shorts or specific tailored trousers for added protection.

>> JERSEYS/JACKETS

Bad weather conditions seem much worse if you do not have the right equipment. Sweat cools on the skin and if your core temperature drops, it can be hard to warm up again. To make things worse, if it is raining and breezy, you have all the right ingredients for a dose of hypothermia. A good breathable wind and waterproof jacket, cut for mountain biking, is

Handy inventions like this shock pump and replacement shock are useful additions to your pack.

when buying a neck brace is getting the correct size and adjustment. Some helmets do not sit as well as others, and it is highly recommended that you seek professional help when sizing and buying a neck brace.

>> ANKLE AND WRIST GUARDS

Anyone suffering from an existing injury to the ankles or wrists may want to use extra support in these areas. Ankles and wrists take huge loads when riding in rough terrain, increasing the potential of damage to ligaments and tendons. There are a few manufacturers who make guards specifically for mountain bikes, but most pharmacies sell strapping and supports for knees, ankles and wrists. Should you have an existing problem, or develop an injury, seek medical advice and rest – riding with injured joints can make the problem worse and prolong recovery time.

>> HYDRATION SYSTEM/PACK AND RECOMMENDED CONTENTS

There are now many types of system out there to choose from, all boasting superior technologies. Choose a size that suits your ride – you may end up owning a few different-sized packs for different rides. As a guideline you should be drinking about one litre of fluid per one hour of exercise. The most popular size hydration packs will hold around the three-litre mark.

You will also need to buy some essential spares and tools to carry in your pack and, once again, tailor your equipment to suit the ride that you are going to undertake. Essential items for your pack are:

- First-aid kit
- Inner tube
- Tyre levers
- Pump
- Patches
- Tyre patch (old plastic toothpaste tube)
- Chain tool
- Chain link (SRAM quick link or Shimano pin)
- Allen keys – multi-tool
- Spare clothes – wind/waterproof jacket
- Spoke key
- Cable ties
- Gaffer tape
- Assortment of bolts/washers/barrel adjusters
- Any specific tools for your bike

>> CHOOSING THE RIGHT TYRE FOR THE JOB

As I have mentioned in previous chapters, there are a multitude of tyre cuts out there, all intended for different conditions. You will also have a choice of different sidewall technologies, tubeless/non-tubeless systems and rubber compounds.

>> CUT

Below is a guide to help you choose the right tyre for different conditions. You will need at least two different sets of tyres for the extremes of weather, depending on where you live and what you ride.

STREET

For those of you riding skate parks and street, a low-profiled tyre will suit all occasions.

- Slick – small cut
- Semi-slick – medium-size side blocks, slick centre and rounded profile

OFF ROAD

Dry weather

- Semi-slick – medium-size side blocks, rounded profile
- Low profile knobby – even blocks
- Medium size knobby – close centre blocks

Dry/damp conditions

- Medium size knobby – large flat edge centre blocks

Intermediate/wet

- Large square blocks with large spacing

Wet weather

- Tall spiked blocks with large spacing for mud clearance

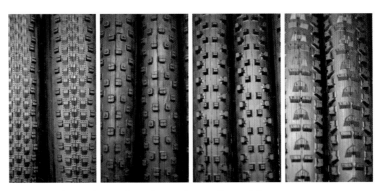

Different tyres suit different terrains and conditions.

>> SIDEWALL

When selecting a tyre you need to consider not only the weather conditions but also the terrain. The robustness of a tyre depends on the sidewall thickness, which will also have an impact on the weight of the tyre. Downhill racers use extra-thick two-ply tyres to deal with the harsh terrain, whereas cross-country riders and racers will use single-ply tyres for minimal rolling resistance and less weight. Single-ply tyres are prone to being cut by sharp rocks, but are considerably lighter than the two-ply variants.

Tyre manufacturers also produce different types of beading – this is the lip that holds the tyre onto the rim. Some tyres will be foldable, where the bead is made from super-tough Kevlar that is lighter than the normal steel bead. They are expensive, but they do save space when it comes to transporting and storing them.

>> TUBELESS/NON-TUBELESS

Then there is the option of a tubeless or a non-tubeless tyre. Once again cost comes into play – tubeless systems are more expensive than standard tyres. A tubeless tyre will have a small rubber wiper on the bead that helps it seal onto the rim. So given all these options we ask the question: what are the advantages of the more expensive tubeless tyre?

A tubeless system will be lighter and therefore has less rolling resistance than a traditional tyre and inner tube setup. The lighter weight means the wheel will accelerate and decelerate faster, and lower pressures can be used for better traction. Lower pressures will, however, reduce the rolling resistance. In my opinion the measurable difference in rolling resistance is minimal, compared to the huge advantage that comes from the additional traction.

Pinch punctures, often sustained when using an inner tube, are not an issue in the tubeless option. A pinch, or snakebite, puncture occurs when the tyre is compressed and contacts the rim – the inner tube is pinched in the gap and can suffer from being pierced. Obviously this problem is removed when the inner tube is removed. The great thing about tubeless rim tyre combos is that you can still use a standard Presta valve inner tube should you tear the sidewall while out in the wilderness.

>> COMPOUND

The final piece to the tyre puzzle will be selecting the right compound. Most manufacturers now produce various compounds for each cut of tyre. Softer compounds are ideal for downhill but the increased rolling resistance make them arduous work for cross-country and all-mountain riding. Once again your selection will depend on where you are riding and the type of surface you will be riding on. Ultimately there will always be a trade-off and a compromise must be made.

>> QUICK GUIDE

Large tyre: Deep tread 2.2–2.5"

Plus:	Minus:
• Better traction	• Increased rolling resistance
• Added suspension	• Heavy

Medium tyre: Medium tread 2.0–2.2"

Plus:	Minus:
• Good traction	• Less grip
• Slight suspension	

Narrow tyre: Low tread 1.5–2.0"

Plus:	Minus:
• Fast rolling	• Less grip
• Light	• Hard to fit
	• Thin sidewall vulnerable to pinch punctures

Folding tyres are light and easier to get on and off the rim.

SKILLS AND TECHNIQUE_

Remember, we need to know how to stop a machine before we start it, we need to go up before we can go down and all things should flow in a chronological order. The development of technological advances in mountain biking came because riders wanted an easier way to get up in the hills for that inevitable blast back down to the bottom. Mountain bike skills should be taught and learned as a progression.

In this chapter I will demonstrate the synchronisation between the techniques and manoeuvres that unlock all the potential of mountain biking. Simply put, we must consider and understand the basic principles of riding:

- Equipment: You, mental and physical – You and your bike, its condition and setup

- Environment: Visual cues and trail input

- Technique: Looking – Speed control, braking, accelerating, pumping – Body position – Footwork

- Equipment: You – Confidence – Control – Commitment

- Environment: Entry – Section – Exit

A mountain bike skill or trick is usually understood to be simply a combination of techniques performed in order. However, mountain biking skills go way beyond jumping and hopping – knowing how to adjust your setup and look after yourself out on the trail are equally important things to learn. A poorly adjusted bike will hinder your ability to ride smoothly in rough terrain and you will get more from your mountain biking experience if your cockpit is set up correctly.

Why is it important to practise skills and technique?

Many riders focus on their fitness and spend huge sums of money on fancy components in an effort to better their performance, but few spend the time to brush up on their skills and perfect their technique. I see (and follow) many people who wing it through trails, riding by the seat of their pants, using brute force and excessive effort to clean the simplest trail sections. They could get far more enjoyment out of their experience if they spent time practising, as opposed to just jumping on the bike and blazing trails. Top riders make it look effortless because basically, when using good technique, it is!

Would you go skiing and not take lessons from a professional?

There is yet another popular misconception that riding a mountain bike is simply riding a bicycle, just off road. The skill set required to ride in a safe, efficient manner in technical terrain is miles apart from that needed to pedal a bicycle around the streets. I see novice riders spend money on bikes and get out there in the wilderness, with no instruction or training, and it pains me to think they are riding in an unsafe manner and could be getting much more out of their experience if they sought professional assistance. The riders of old have paved the way and we can help you take a shortcut past the school of hard knocks and essentially progress your riding much faster and safer.

When we use good technique we save energy and cheat the trail using gravity and momentum to aid our progress, not hinder it. The bonus here is you have more in the tank to spend when you need to. By being efficient and smooth you are able to ride further and faster. Taking hits from the trail and hitting opposing obstacles like square edges take energy out of you, in terms of both forward progression and all-important calories. Spending time and money on learning skills is far more beneficial in improving your riding than shelling out on a fancy set of wheels. Get the basics down and see for yourself just how much more your mountain bike experience opens up.

Even if you are a seasoned rider there are some key techniques laid out in this chapter that will help you get more bang for your bucks. Mountain biking is a skill-based sport and can be learned in a progressive manner in a safe environment. Diversify your riding and try not to be in a hurry to hit the trail each time you ride – set aside some time during your ride to practise, practise, practise. With a little imagination, a seemingly boring forest road section can be turned into a playground.

◎ **TIP**

By using good technique you can ride faster with more control.

>> PREFLIGHT INSPECTION

Before we head out on the trail we should give our bike a quick check over to make sure that there are no loose or worn components that could affect the way it performs. You should also carry out a routine service on your bike – this will help you get the optimum ride and avoid unnecessary expenditure on replacing worn or failed parts. Get a trained mechanic to handle things that you are unsure about – the last thing you need is a huge stack that could have been avoided. By looking after your bike you will have the comfort of knowing that it is able to carry you up mountains and back down them safely, allowing you to concentrate on your riding.

Don't be shy here. Grab things, shake things and have a good visual inspection of your equipment. Tighten and/or adjust accordingly. Should you find a component that is excessively worn you should attend to it before you hit the trail.

Make sure your wheels are tight and check that the lever is closed nice and tight (it should leave an imprint in your skin when closed with the palm). Try not to over-tighten it as this will stress the metal and stretch the threads, reducing their effectiveness.

Should the lever get stuck the fork leg will stop it from spinning round – there is also adequate room to get your hand behind the lever.

◎ FRONT WHEEL LEVER

The lever on your front wheel should point either upwards or rearwards. Avoid closing it against the fork leg as you will not be able to get a good grip on it should you need to undo it. This is particularly important in cold weather conditions. Bolt-through systems need to be checked too. Once again avoid over-tightening the small Allen bolts as they are likely to sheer or pull the soft aluminium thread out of the fork stanchion.

◎ REAR WHEEL LEVER

Your rear quick-release lever should point rearwards to avoid being smashed on rocks or hooked on vegetation. This also enables you to get a good grip around the lever to undo it. Never have it pointing downwards – it could hit rocks and would be moved in the direction that loosens it.

Here we can also see good access to the lever. Should you drop on to a rock it may loosen and if this happens you should stop to check your bike for damage.

Check your seat quick-release to make sure it is not going to impale you if you crash. It should be tight enough so the post does not drop or move round easily, but avoid over-tightening it. Once again the component parts will be stressed if you do this.

Now grab the saddle and try to rotate it. Move it up and down by holding the nose and tail, just to make sure it is not loose on its clamp. Make sure that there are no rips or splits in the saddle and that the rails are not bent.

Make sure your saddle is in a good position and tight on the post.

Grab your bars and try to twist them. If they move it could be because either your grips are moving or the stem bolts need tightening up. Do not over-tighten stem bolts and when doing them up, work on opposites, tightening the diagonal ones first. Make sure the gap between the clamps is even all round.

While you're looking at the bars, grab your brake and gear levers and see if they are tight. Back in the old days we used to run our brake levers a little loose so they would move and not dent our top tubes. Nowadays, though, frame design and different geometry mean this is a rare occurrence. I still run my brake levers so I can move them by hand. It doesn't take a lot of effort to move them and that helps in saving the lever blades when the bike hits the floor in a crash; they can also move if they come into contact with me during a crash.

Stand in front of your bike and grip the front wheel between your thighs. Now try to move the bars clockwise and anticlockwise – hopefully the stem does not spin round.

Moving down below the stem we have the headset. We need to check if it is tight and there is no play in the bearings. Lift the front wheel in the air and turn the bars/wheel left and right. If it is tight then the bearings are under too much load or are excessively worn; if there is a tight spot then you have a bent steerer tube on your forks. The movement should be quiet and easy – a rough feeling and typically noisy headset either has a lack of grease or is worn out and pitted.

Now place the wheel on the floor and stand behind the bars, above your bike. Apply the front brake and rock the bike backwards and forwards. While you are doing this, place your hand around the top race and feel for play – if you can feel movement then the headset is loose. Repeat the process with the lower race. On modern bikes you may feel a slight movement from either the fork stanchions or the pad moving in your disc brake calliper. To help eliminate this, turn the wheel to 90 degrees and rock the bike without using the brake. You can also rest the front wheel against a wall and rock the frame.

Check your tyres for pressure and wear. Make sure that the knobs are not splitting away and that there are no bulges or rips in the sidewall.

Lift your front wheel, give it a spin, look and listen. A wheel that does not spin freely and effortlessly will slow you down on the trail and cause excessive calories to be burned. If the wheel slows down quickly or does not spin freely it could be caused by your brakes rubbing, or else by your hub having been over-tightened or suffering from worn, seized bearings. Grab the tyre and rock the wheel left to right. If there is movement either the quick-release is loose (you should have checked this and therefore eliminated this possibility already) or, more likely, the hub is worn and/or loose. Run your hand round the spokes, plucking them to make sure you have no loose spokes. Take a good look at the rims to make sure there are no dents or cracks, spin them up and look for buckles and flat spots.

Repeat the same with the rear wheel, remembering to spin it in the direction of drive so it will freewheel.

Spin your cranks round and rock them from side to side. Ensure that they spin freely and have no play.

Spin your pedals round, making sure that they too spin freely and have no play.

Carry out a visual inspection of brake hoses and gear cables. Make sure that there are no splits or leaks in hydraulic systems and no splits or frays in gear cable outers and inners. Take a good, close look, as they

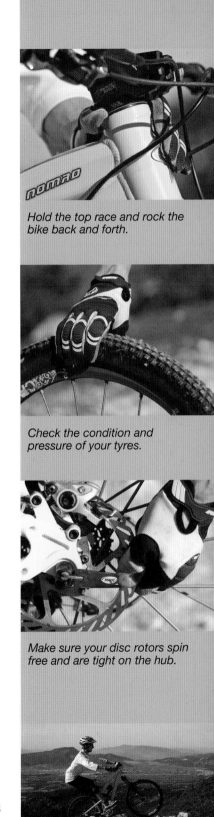

Hold the top race and rock the bike back and forth.

Check the condition and pressure of your tyres.

Make sure your disc rotors spin free and are tight on the hub.

Check that your cranks and pedals spin free and have no play.

Keep an eye on the amount of wear your brake pads have and look out for uneven pad wear. If this happens you need to align your calliper so it is square to the disc rotor.

often split near the shifter, mech or wherever they pass pivots on full-suspension bikes.

Take a good look at the brake pads. On bikes equipped with rim brakes you need to make sure that the brake block is not rubbing on the tyre, or going to miss the rim and go in the spokes. Ensure that the whole pad contacts the rim. For disc brakes, check for pad wear and the condition of your brake rotors. Make sure that there are no leaks and that the rotor is straight and firmly secured onto the hub.

Check your drive system for wear and lubricate your chain if necessary, but use lubricant sparingly. Avoid using non-specific lubricants, as they are often too viscous and attract dirt to the chain, increasing the wear. Wet-weather riding will eat into components and keeping your drive system dirt-free will increase the longevity of your equipment and make that winter bash a more enjoyable experience. Try to avoid running an old chain on a new cassette and vice versa. Worn drive components should be replaced to avoid damage to other components in the drive train.

Check that your gears are working and you can move the shifter easily and get a nice, smooth shift. You should replace your gear cables on a regular basis to ensure you get a smooth, light, concise shift. Obviously if you ride 20 miles every day of the week, you will be replacing parts more often than someone who just goes out for a 10-mile ride at the weekend. Look after your bike and it will look after you.

Check the condition of your chain and drive system.

Suspension units should be checked for leaks around the dust wipers and adjusters. For air systems, check the pressure at regular intervals. Move the back end around to check for loose pivots and swing links.

>> SETTING UP THE COCKPIT

There are multiple adjustments we can make to our bikes and each one will affect your riding stance in various ways. Subtle changes to brake-lever angle, for instance, will have a dramatic effect on your body position and neutral stance, resulting in more or less control. When making changes to your setup it is a good idea to mark the position of a component, where possible, before making the change. This way you have a reference point to compare with, or refer back to should you not like the change. With all adjustments and skills, start small.

>> BAR ADJUSTMENTS

BAR LENGTH

Longer bars have been adopted by downhill riders and the trend has crossed over into the all-mountain and cross-country scene. Wider bars give greater control at higher speeds and lower the chest towards the stem, putting more weight over the front end and onto the front wheel. They do, however, give a clumsier ride than shorter ones at slower speeds in rough terrain. There will be a cut-off point depending on the width of your shoulders. Bear in mind, wider bars will distribute the loads from bump forces into different muscle groups in the arms and shoulders. Cross-country racers still use flat bars that are quite a bit shorter than downhill bars; they are also made from lighter materials to help keep weight to a minimum. Choose the correct bar for the job to avoid any nasty surprises.

SWEEP/RISE

A riser bar will come in a certain sweep (the angle that the bar curves towards you) and a certain rise. Unfortunately, it's only through trial and error that you will find a sweep and a rise that meet your requirements and feel right – try to borrow some riser bars from friends before you buy. Further adjustments can be made by altering the angle at which you clamp the bars into the stem. As a rough guide, the riser section between the two curves should be in the vertical position when viewed from the side. The grip area should sweep upwards and rearwards slightly.

By rolling the bar forwards you increase the lift potential (ability to lift the weight from this lever point) and move your body weight over the front end more, subtle though the difference is. By rolling it backwards you will be riding in the rear half more. Both forward and rearward rotation at the extremes will decrease the lift.

>> STEM ADJUSTMENTS

Different stem lengths will alter the lift – a basic bit of physics will prove my point. Try lifting a reasonable weight attached to a handlebar with your arms stretched out in front of you. Then try the same again with your arms slightly bent and lowered closer to your torso. The shorter the stem, the more lift you will have. However, this position puts you more upright and removes weight from the front wheel. The steering response on a shorter stem is also faster, but go too short and you may find things a little on the lively side.

Think about racing cars and their small steering wheels – small inputs at the steering wheel equal large movements at the wheels. Then compare this to a bus – the driver wrestles a large steering wheel where he or she has to make large inputs to get small movement at the wheels. The same applies for stems lengths – small inputs to a short stem cause a big change to the angle of the front wheel, whereas a longer stem requires more movement to get the same result. Bar width will also have the same results. Narrower handlebars make a bike twitchy and a small input through the bar has a big output at the front wheel. Longer bars slow down the steering response and give greater control at high speeds in rough terrain.

Stem height can also be adjusted by moving the spacers on the steerer tube so that they sit below or above the clamp. You can also choose to run a stem with different degrees of rise. A stem with a flat zero-degree rise will help get weight over the front wheel, whereas a higher-rise stem will reduce this effect and put you in a more upright riding position and your weight back onto the rear half of the bike. Once again by trial and error you will find the setup that feels right – borrow components and ride other people's setups, making note of the size and angles before you splash out on new components.

>> BRAKE LEVER POSITION: INBOARD/OUTBOARD ANGLE

Your brake levers should be in such a position that you can rest your first finger in the cup or hook shape at the end of the lever. This gives you maximum control over the lever, allowing you to feed the brake on

With your bike on an even surface view the bar from the end. The riser section should shift around the vertical and the ends should sweep backwards and slightly upwards.

A correction pen is ideal for marking your base measure.

smoothly and steadily. The angle of the lever has been under debate for some time and I have to say there is an element of personal preference to consider here. I am a firm believer that the old way of lining up the lever, with a straight arm and extended fingers, is not exactly right.

First we have to decide where over the bike we are when we set up the angle – sitting, standing, leaning forwards or just off the back? All these positions will create different angles between your wrist and the lever. As we use our brakes mostly when descending, it makes sense to be stood tall and proud over the bike in our neutral stance (see the basic riding skills later in this chapter for the neutral stance) to make the adjustment. You should have your wrists dipped to push and drive the bike forwards. Think about this angle for a moment. How would you push a heavy shopping cart? With your wrists straight, dipped or rolled forwards? Hopefully, you would dip the wrist and push through with your palms at about 45 degrees.

Downhill riders have drawn experience from motocross and now run their brake levers much flatter to help with dipping the wrist and driving through. If you set everything up in-line, as per the old way of doing things, you open up the potential of your hand slipping forwards off the bars when you take hits from the front.

Try this simple experiment with a friend. Grip the bar with your wrist pushed forwards, get your friend to slap your arm just behind the wrist from below in an effort to knock your hand off the handlebar. Make a note of how much effort is required, then repeat the process with your wrist in-line and with your wrist dipped. I am sure you will achieve the same result that was a concluding piece of evidence for myself in this conundrum – a dipped wrist position provides a better grip than when your wrist is in-line.

I have found that certain combinations of gear shifter and brake lever make it easier or harder to get that nice sweet spot where your levers are far enough in so that you can get some purchase on the end of the blade and still reach your gear shifter. You might have to find a compromise here, but the importance of being able to slow down and control your speed safely outweighs being able to shift efficiently.

A further adjustment you can make to the brake lever is the reach. Most setups have a small grub screw or a dial that moves the lever blade in towards the bar or away from it. The reach should be adjusted so that you are not overstretching to reach the lever, but you are not so close that the lever hits the grip before the brake is fully on (you will find an element of sponginess to the latter part of the lever travel).

You can buy spacers of varying thickness that will help you get the right set up.

By lifting our levers we gain more control over the bike and can drive it through rough terrain. This also helps us scoop the bar from underneath while covering the brake.

Adjust the reach so you are not over-stretched or crushing your finger.

>> SADDLE ADJUSTMENTS: HEIGHT, ANGLE AND FORE/AFT

Here we have multiple adjustments we can make, including height, angle and fore/aft. Let's start with getting your seat at the correct height for pedalling (if you ride street, free-ride or downhill this is not so important). Sit on your bike and lean against a wall so both feet are on the pedals. Drop one pedal so that the cranks run in line with your seat tube, just off the vertical. Now place the lower foot so that the heel is on the pedal – your leg should be nearly locked out, but do not overstretch or hyperextend the knee.

This gives you a ballpark starting position from which you may wish to raise the post (to increase pedal efficiency) or lower the post (for more clearance and stability) by a few millimetres. Mountain biking, done efficiently and effectively, requires you to be out of the saddle and to stand on the pedals for a considerable length of time, so running your seat just shy of the mark is no bad thing. However, do not go to extremes as you will open up the potential of knee damage and other muscular dysfunction.

Downhill, free-riders and street riders will opt for running their seats much lower to assist with clearance, which allows them to move around on the bike more and suck up large bumps. To perform certain skills, like the manual (see skills section), it is better to have your seat lower, as you need to move around in the area where your seat would be if it were set at normal pedal-efficient height. If you are a downhiller you will need to pedal at some point and, over long, flat sections, you may need to sit down to aid recovery. For this reason it is important to maintain some level of pedal efficiency so try to avoid putting your seat too low.

Once you have set the correct height it's time to set the seat angle. Guys may want to tilt the nose up just ever so slightly from level, whereas ladies may prefer to dip the nose slightly to avoid chafing. All adjustments should be made from the starting point of your seat running parallel to the floor, with your bike on a flat surface. See what suits you best and avoid angles that are at the extremes.

Now you have the desired height and angle let's make the final adjustment. The fore and aft position is set by sliding the saddle forwards and backwards on its rails on the post. This adjustment will affect the path that your knees take when pedalling. It is very important not to adjust your reach by the saddle fore and aft movement – this adjustment should be done by changing the stem and not by moving the saddle.

To get the saddle in the correct position you need to be sitting on your bike, leaning against a wall. Move the cranks so they are level (parallel to the floor), with the balls of your feet over the pedal axles. Now sight a line

Make sure the nose points forwards in line with the top tube.

The leg should be straight, but not locked out when the crank is vertical and the heel is on the pedal.

Set the correct fore/aft by visualising a vertical line up from the pedal axle through your knee.

down from the centre of the knee of the lead foot – this should run through the pedal axle. I cannot stress enough how important this adjustment is. If you're seated too far back or forward, and the knee does not line up over the pedal axle, the result will be that the knee moves in a cam sort of motion. This will erode the soft tissue on the back of the kneecap and can lead to knee problems over time.

Check the bolts are tight after setting the angle.

◎ TIP

Gents' saddles are usually quite narrow and ladies may wish to opt for a female-specific saddle, which is wider and offers more support to the pelvic girdle.

Make sure the cranks are evenly spaced.

◎ **TIP**

By riding with flat pedals you will learn good technique and not cheat a lift by pulling up on the pedals.

>> CRANKS: LENGTH AND OFFSET

Complete bikes will usually come with standard 170mm or 175mm crank arms, but if you are building a bike there are other options. Smaller riders will opt for shorter 165mm or 170mm arms, whereas taller guys and girls will go for 175mm or monster 180mm cranks. The shorter arms give more ground clearance and stand-over height; you are also not so stretched out when cruising in the neutral stance, giving more control. The downsides to shorter arms are less leverage and increased cadence (revolutions per minute). Some downhill riders will use shorter crank arms to give more clearance on bikes that are built with low bottom brackets.

With a new bike that is bought complete or built by a professional there will be no issues with the offset and Q-factor (width between the pedals). For those of you building up new bikes or repairing old ones make sure that you check the offset of the cranks. Measure from the back of each arm to the seat tube to ensure that the cranks are centred. There are small spacers provided with new upgrade and replacement parts to allow you to do this. If in doubt get a professional mechanic to do the job for you. A few millimetres at the bottom bracket equals a large displacement in the hips, so make sure that the cranks are even or you could incur problems with muscle groups and joints.

>> PEDALS: TENSION FOR CLIP-IN PEDALS

Clip-in pedals give us extra pedalling efficiency over flat pedals, but a novice rider can soon be scared off by not being able to unclip and thus falling over when coming to a stop. Most pedals will have an Allen bolt that allows you to adjust the tension of the springs. Start with the spring tension at its weakest. If you are using good technique you will not suffer from accidental unclipping and you can increase the tension as your confidence builds. Make sure that your cleats are tight and square, as loose cleats could twist and you will be stuck to the pedal, while badly aligned cleats could result in damage to the ankles, knees and hip joints.

>> SUSPENSION

Now that the cockpit is adjusted correctly we need to set up the suspension, which includes the tyre pressure as well. Hard-tails and fully rigid bikes still have suspension – tyres deflect when we roll over rough ground and add an element of shock absorption. I used to run quite large tyres on my hard-tails to help eliminate any trail buzz, the noise created by high-frequency bumps.

>> TYRE PRESSURE

This is another area where trial and error will come into play. Most tyres have a recommended pressure written on the side that will give a good guideline. Softer pressures will roll slower but give a greater contact patch and therefore offer more grip. You may encounter pinch punctures if using inner tubes and running low pressures – tubeless systems will not suffer from this problem, but the likelihood of denting the rim is increased with low pressures. At a downhill race event you will see riders constantly adjusting pressures during practice, in an effort to find the optimum setup for the given conditions. Cross-country trail riders typically choose a desired pressure and stick with it in all conditions. Rider style will dictate your desired setup and it is a matter of personal preference.

◎ TIP

Remember, suspension needs to be set up and tested in a realistic trail environment. Bouncing up and down in a car park does not replicate hits coming from below when on the trail. Think about the physics here – it is the force from a hit that pushes the wheel up into the suspension units and through its travel. This hit is working against the resistance, pressure or weight of your body and your bike. The suspension unit then needs enough force to drive the wheel back down on the far side of the bump.

When the terrain has a hole, the suspension unit needs to be able to react fast enough and drive our wheels down into it, rather than the whole vehicle (you and your bike) dropping into it to then actuate the suspension as it takes the hit on the far side of the hole. The only time your mass impacts on the suspension unit from above is when you become slightly weightless in a free-fall situation. In this case, when the bike contacts the floor your mass acts on top of that by impacting as well, after a momentary delay.

Your tyre offers a large amount of suspension.

Check the pressure by pushing down on the contact patch.

Although the surface is rough our core should follow a smooth virtual line.

◎ **TIP**

Refer to the owner's manual or data online for details of your suspension unit.

>> ADJUSTING SUSPENSION FORKS

Depending on the type of fork you have there will be some adjustments that can be made to improve the performance of the unit. Most basic forks have a simple compression and rebound adjustment; the more expensive versions come with clever valving systems, allowing you to make even more adjustments to the ride quality.

SETTING UP PRE-LOAD AND SAG/DROOP

First things first – we must set the air pressure or spring weight so the fork sits in its travel. This allows the fork to drop (droop) into holes, rather than the front wheel falling in before actuating the travel. Too much sag and you will blow through the travel on the smallest hit, too little and you will not get the optimum ride. Lighter riders sometimes find it hard to obtain spring weights low enough to get efficient use from a fork. If this is the case you may want to go for lighter air forks that allow you to run lower pressures and get the optimum sag.

Coil springs can be changed out by removing a top cap. There are various ways to remove them – make sure you use the correct tools or get a professional mechanic to do it for you. Air forks are easier to adjust and will have a Schrader valve at one end of the fork leg, to attach a shock pump.

Some branded forks will have a rubber ring on the fork stanchion – this is to assist with measuring travel. Another way to measure this is with a cable tie, but you should be careful when using these as they may press on the fork seal when the fork bottoms out. As a rough guide we're looking for about 20 per cent of the travel being taken up on cross-country setups and up to 40 per cent on downhill bikes.

The measurement is taken when you are standing on the bike in the neutral stance. Lean against a tree or wall and let the bike settle, then slide the rubber ring or cable tie to the seal and carefully step off the bike. This is a tricky process and you may want to get someone to help you. Try measuring the sag when you are standing over the bike, with your weight being distributed through your feet via the pedals and cranks. Then try measuring it when sitting on the seat. You may prefer a stiffer setup than others – make small adjustments and ride the same section of trail, again and again, to feel the difference. You should have your fork set soft enough that on big hits you bottom them out. The travel is there, use it!

I increase my rebound adjustment when running lower pressures or lighter spring weights, to help eliminate the suspension unit blowing through its travel too quickly. Repetitive hits will stack up which means the bike will have an increased tendency to go through its travel faster.

◎ TIP

The concept of a bike suspension unit is to keep the vehicle (you and your bike) level while your wheels move independently up and down over undulating terrain.

COMPRESSION

Some suspension units will have crude methods for adjusting the compression, whereas the more expensive versions will have multiple adjustments. The points covered above apply to adjusting compression on more basic models – a softer fork will compress faster, whereas a stiffer

Check your owners manual for specific setup guidelines.

Some forks come with a handy O ring to help you measure travel.

one will compress slower. Set the fork too soft and it will move quickly through its compression; set it harder and it will move less quickly.

On more expensive forks the speed of this movement can be adjusted independently via a dial or internal valves. This extra adjustment means you can run a stiffer fork that will still move faster through its travel, or run a softer fork that will move slower through the stroke. This additional adjustment helps you to fine-tune the fork to suit your riding style. Taking this a step further we have slow-speed and high-speed adjustments. Some forks allow even more fine-tuning and you can control how fast the fork moves through its travel on slow-speed hits (deep rounded holes/slow-speed riding on very rough terrain) and on larger, high-speed hits (the big boulder that leaps out in front of you, causing the fork to compress very quickly).

REBOUND

Once the fork has been adjusted for your rider weight and to take the hits, we need to adjust how fast it returns to its original position via the rebound adjuster. The rebound dial will make the fork return faster or slower, depending on your compression adjustment – we need to dial this in to balance the fork. Faster compression rates will suit a slightly slower rebound (you will be bouncing around all over the place if you run both fast compression and fast rebound). Slower, more squishy, compression setups work better with a slightly faster rebound (the fork will sit too far in the travel and stack down through multiple bumps if a slow rebound is set).

TRAVEL

Cross-country and all-mountain forks sometimes come with travel adjusters on the top of a fork leg. By lowering the fork you will steepen the head angle, increasing the responsiveness and assisting in climbing (bikes with tall forks and slack angles will want to wheelie on steep climbs). This is a handy addition and another adjustment that helps you set your bike up at its optimum for various types of terrain.

LOCK OUT

Another great addition to modern suspension forks has been the introduction of a lock-out system – a plain and simple device, often bar-mounted, that allows you to lock out the fork, making it a rigid structure. This really assist riders when climbing out of the saddle. The forces created from your efforts can be absorbed through the fork and your energy soaked up. By locking the fork your energy goes into all-important forward motion and is not wasted through fork movement. Some systems have clever dials that help by limiting the responsiveness of the fork – they require, more or less, bump force to open the valving inside and actuate the movement.

◎ FORK QUICK GUIDE

Red = Rebound

Blue = Compression/Sensitivity

Note: Different manufacturers may colour code in different manners.

A bar mounted lock out lever makes for easy adjustment on the move, but it does make the cockpit look cluttered.

>> REAR SUSPENSION

Shock absorbers have similar adjustments to forks – compression rebound and intelligent valving systems allow you to fine-tune your setup. I am a firm believer in getting value for money from your purchase and that goes right down to obtaining full travel from your suspension. I see bikes patter across the surface, as most people run their suspension too firm, but we need to keep our tyres stuck to the ground for optimum traction in every direction. A bike that patters is losing grip, not only when braking but also when accelerating and turning.

Sure, there is a downside to a supple, soft setup and you have to set up your bike for the specific task in hand. Cross-country riders need to be efficient, and energy wasted through suspension unit movement is not aiding their forward motion. Downhill racers and riders, however, will benefit from better grip and can sacrifice some efficiency and run softer, more supple setups. For those of you trail riding and just out having fun, you may find a slightly softer bike more arduous, but the increased grip and traction will open up new possibilities and inevitably lead to faster, safer riding.

A cable operated remote lock out.

Titanium springs are light and offer a plush responsive ride. This Boss shock with its dainty spring is only a few grams heavier than an equivalent travel air shock.

Air shock absorbers are lighter than standard steel coil spring options.

Soft compounds grip well, but are heavy going on the legs.

TYPES OF SHOCK ABSORBER

- **Coil sprung:** A basic oil chamber, with valving to control the flow of oil, and an external coil spring. More expensive versions will have extra valving systems to assist with pedalling efficiency and to help control compression and rebound rates. Some manufacturers use air (nitrogen gas) chambers to allow fine-tuning of the compression rate.

- **Air:** An air chamber that deals with the process of controlling compression rebound. It may have extra valving systems to assist in the control of the compression rate and rebound.

◎ SHOCK ABSORBER QUICK GUIDE

Red = Rebound

Blue = Compression/Pro Pedal/Bottom out

Note: Different manufacturers may colour code in different manners.

SETTING UP PRE-LOAD AND SAG/DROOP

The longer the stroke on the shock, the more travel you have and the softer you can run your bike. This is once again an area of huge debate and like most setup adjustments there will always be a level of personal preference that comes into play.

Sit on your bike and repeat the same process as described in the fork setup (page 123). Measure the amount of travel the shock goes through and refer to comparisons in table 6.1 for percentage sag corresponding to your discipline. Here you should see a larger percentage difference in the measures being taken while standing up on the pedals and while sitting down in the saddle. When we sit we create extra leverage through the saddle seat post and seat tube, compared to when we have our weight being transferred through the pedals' crank arms and bottom bracket axle.

Table 6.1: Percentage sag

Bike type	Sag (%)
XC race	10–20
XC trail ride	15–40
All-mountain	20–50
Downhill	20–50

Depending on the type of riding you are doing, set your bike up accordingly. If you are descending standing up then use the standing method to measure sag. For those of you doing distance rides and spending more time in the saddle and less up on the pedals, set up your sag while in the seated position. Trail riders will spend time in both positions so you can set up the bike between the two points. It should be noted that the distance between the two will be minimal on the shock, but hugely exaggerated at the axle. Be as precise and scientific as you can if you want to get the most out of your equipment.

© TIP

Consider the fact that if you do not experiment with different setups then you limit the possibilities of finding the optimum setup that feels right for you. It is through direct experience that we discover what suits us best as individuals.

Shock absorbers have to deal with bump force and the force from the bike and the rider on landings. Some shock absorbers have separate controls for bottom out.

COMPRESSION

The rate of compression can be adjusted by increasing the air pressure or changing the spring weight (or a combination of the two). Higher pressures and stiffer springs will require more effort to move the shock through its travel. A specialist tuning company will be able to make changes to internal valving to perfect your setup.

REBOUND

Cheap shock absorber units really don't deserve to be called shock absorbers and offer no rebound control. Good shock absorbers cost for a reason – external dials are there to help you to get that optimum setup with ease. Faster rebound should be applied when running your shock softer, and slower speeds should be used when running your setup with higher compression rates. High-frequency bumps require faster rebound compared to longer, larger, slower hits. There will ultimately have to be an element of compromise when choosing just one setup, and if you find you are being bucked up on large compressions then slow down the rebound.

TRAVEL

Travel can be limited by increasing air pressure or spring weight, but this will make the ride harsh, as it ups the compression rate. The only real solution is to have the shock modified by a specialist, who will change the shock stroke length, reducing the available travel.

LOCK OUT

To help combat input through pedalling, top-end shocks have on-the-fly lock-out adjustments. A dial will change the valving and necessary bump force that is required to actuate the shock, a very useful tool for that all-round trail bike.

Table 6.2: Suspension troubleshooting

Problem	Fork and shock absorber	Tyres
Sliding in the turns	Soften your suspension	Soften your tyre pressure Change to a more aggressive cut Use a softer compound
Skidding excessively over braking bumps	Soften your suspension Increase rebound speed	Soften the rear tyre pressure Change to a more aggressive cut Use a softer compound
Wheel spin on climbs	Soften your suspension	Soften the rear tyre pressure Change to a more aggressive cut Use a softer compound
Sitting on the floor, dragging your heels	Stiffen your suspension Increase the compression rate	
Feeling like you are pulling a car tyre	Stiffen your suspension	Increase your tyre pressure Change to a narrower low profile tyre Use a harder compound
Getting bucked up on large compressions (typically from transitions on jumps)	Slow rebound speed	
Bottoming out too frequently	Increase the spring weight/air pressure (increase the compression rate)	
The ride feels harsh	Soften spring weight/decrease air pressure (decrease compression rate)	Soften your tyre pressure
Getting lots of punctures – snakebite/pinch flats	Soften your suspension	Increase your tyre pressure Change to a wider tyre with thicker sidewall
Denting your wheel rims	Soften your suspension	Increase your tyre pressure Change to a wider tyre with thicker sidewall

◎ TIP

Always read the owner's manual and abide by the manufacturer's operating guidelines/parameters. Seek professional assistance if you are unsure of what you are doing. Badly adjusted suspension could affect the bike's handling capabilities and may result in failure or injury.

>> BACK 2 BASICS – CORE RIDING SKILLS AND TECHNIQUES

SKILL 1: THE ART OF STOPPING – SPEED CONTROL

Before we operate any piece of machinery we must familiarise ourselves with its component parts and the essential parts that stop the machine. For us mountain bikers that of course means our brakes, but the art of stopping is shrouded in myths and misconceptions. The scariest thing I hear people say is to avoid using the front brakes as you may fly over the handlebars. Sure, this may be the case if you just grabbed a strong handful of front brake but few of you, I hope, would envisage doing so. The laws of physics will give you all the answers you need to fully understand that your front brake is not only the most efficient but also the safest way to control your speed. There will always be exceptions to rules and top-end riders will cheat the system and use controlled braking in unusual circumstances. For most of you, though, hopefully you will never end up at such odd angles, carrying so much speed that you need to do this.

So to get you started let's look at how we address the lever. From the bike setup section we can see that by moving the levers inboard, we can hook our first finger on the end of the lever blade. This allows your middle finger to maintain a strong grip on the bar (if you have strong hands you can ride by just gripping in this way for a considerable time in rough terrain). By holding the end of the lever, not only do you have the most amount of available leverage, quite literally at your fingertip, but you also have ultimate control. The lever blade will go through a longer arc at the end, as opposed to somewhere closer to the pivot. This in turn enables you to have greater/finer control over how much brake you feed in. We must remember to train the fingers and feel the bars and levers (you also remove the potential of crushing your own fingers by not using your index finger).

The most efficient part of braking happens at the initial contact of the pad with the disc (or block with the rim). Around 75 per cent of the stopping power comes from this initial contact; beyond that the brake becomes more inefficient as heat builds up. This is how ABS works more efficiently than a standard system on motorcars. By using what was formerly referred to as 'cadence braking', we slow the vehicle in a shorter distance because we are being more efficient.

So cadence braking can help slow your bike?

Yes it can, and on long descents this becomes very apparent. If you are suffering from brake fade it may well be that you are dragging the brakes, which is a bad idea – the excessive temperature is making them inefficient. Just remember to feed the brake in slowly.

Other than causing brake fade, dragging the brakes increases pad wear and the additional heat in the system will deteriorate the fluid at a faster rate. There are other factors, like leaking olives (small brass tubes compressed onto the brake) and seals, that can also contribute towards the unnerving scenario of brake fade.

There are more scientific reasons why we should avoid dragging the brakes as we enter the realm of centrifugal force. When we apply the brakes it unsettles the balance of the bike. The forces that act on the wheels through pads contacting discs have a negative effect – wheels become light and want to right themselves when we are leaning over to either side. Try holding your wheel in the air and get a friend to spin it up. While it is whizzing round grab the rear brake lever – you should feel it try to kick the back end of the bike up. The reaction may be ever so slight but it is still proof that science as we know it is still working today. By the way, this is how motocross riders help in influencing the bike's movement while clearing monstrous jumps.

The front tyre deforms as the loads of the rider's mass is transferred through it under extreme braking.

BRAKING TEST

- Find a suitable safe location that has a slight downward incline and a good surface (no loose rocks or slippery roots).

- Mark a line lower down the slope and walk up about 100m (the evidence will vary depending on this distance and the gradient). Mark a second line – this will act as your start line.

- From here, roll back down the hill and at the lower line start braking using only the rear brake. Your aim is to stop as soon as possible without locking the rear wheel, i.e. skidding.

- Mark the spot where you have stopped and now walk back up to the start (it's advisable to do a few runs to help get a feel for the brakes).

- When you are confident you are ready and have settled into smooth braking, try a run but this time use only the front brake. Be sure not to grab at the brake – feed it in slowly. You may need to move slightly to the rear from centre due to the increased load, as your mass above the vehicle will want to move forwards. This is due to the resistance created from your front tyre being pressured into the trail). Remember to mark your stopping point each time.

Hopefully after a few runs you will see the difference for yourself.

There are other things we can look at which emphasise the point that the front brake is the most efficient. Just look at your bike – the front brake rotor is larger than the back one and your rear wheel is no more than a trailer, happily rattling along behind you. The rear axle is located behind the main mass of the vehicle and pilot. You drag this along behind you, so to speak, and your mass has little impact on it.

There is, of course, a problem in certain situations and the rear brake does become the lever of choice to reach for, but contrary to the myth we will not fly over the handlebars if we use our front brake in steep terrain. Examples of rear-only braking would be when we are travelling exceptionally fast and/or encounter ice or we are riding on steep off-camber gradients covered in ice. That really is about it.

In all other situations, we use both brakes together and independently, making quick, controlled movements, increasing and decreasing pressure as the trail surface changes below our tyres. For example, when crossing roots on wet surfaces we will decrease or remove totally the front brake effort as the front wheel passes over the root. There may be a subtle increase in the rear brake effort to help compensate but, as soon as the front wheel is back on a good surface, the front brake is fed back in. Simultaneously, just before the rear wheel comes into contact with said root, we release pressure on the rear brake and, if our front wheel is still on a good surface, increase the front brake effort to compensate. The whole thing is a constant adjustment and balance in an effort to slow the bike or maintain a preferential speed as we descend. It is a very dynamic process and a skill that really does develop and improve with time and exposure.

BRAKING ON DIFFERENT SURFACES AND ON DIFFERENT GRADIENTS – MORE MYTH BUSTING

Another horrible old myth that we need to address is the debate as to whether we should be fully off the back of the bike when descending on steep gradients. This is not the case – if we drop off the back too far, not only do we hyperextend our limbs and eliminate our ability to steer and lean the bike, but we also remove our mass from the wheel that is slowing us in a safe, controlled manner. Hit a rock or root with hyperextended arms and we'll be pinballed off them. When we are so far back we have nothing more to give and, if the gradient gets steeper, we risk free-falling from way back with no way of absorbing the impact when we land. You will be amazed at how steep an incline you can ride down and, remaining centred over the bike, not be ejected over the bars.

You need to release the brake slightly if the rear wheel locks.

◎ **TIP**

As long as we do not meet a square opposing edge that we cannot roll over, we will not be ejected over the bars.

◎ **TIP**

Remember – feed the brake in slowly.

- Monitor your speed on the entry and look down the trail spotting your line.

- Dip the wrists and heels, stay relaxed and cover the brakes.

- Remain focused and relaxed, dip slightly into the rear of the bike and increase your braking force. Stay centred.

- As you approach the steepening gradient get ready to squash the bike down.

- Drive the bike forward and through, remain focused on your exit.

- Return to centre.

- Adjust your speed and ride out clean.

Loose surfaces

Loose surfaces need constant adjustment of the technique, as small rocks lying on hard surfaces will roll under your wheels. By dipping the heels and wrists, we help drive the bike into the ground, forcing the tyres to bite harder in the process. Stay relaxed – being supple is key to letting the bike move around and find traction. Being compliant like a fresh, green piece of wood will help you snake through slippery boulders and loose surfaces like sand. Think about the old, dead branch of a tree – stiff and brittle, it will snap with ease, whereas that newer, green piece of timber will flex. Ask yourself, which tree would you rather be?

Braking bumps

Braking bumps are a by-product of people dragging their brakes and riding a consistent line, and suspension bikes being set up too hard. They are a big bugbear for trail builders as they require constant maintenance. Trail designers now compensate for this behaviour when building trails, by controlling a rider's speed into a section so they are not braking hard into a turn. When a bike is set up too hard it will patter across the surface, and the unweighting of a wheel allows it to lock momentarily, dragging material with it. As the wheel comes light the brake grabs harder as the load on the wheel is decreased, giving the brake more stopping power.

There are a few things we can do to avoid the unpleasant experience of bouncing around through braking bumps. The easiest and most obvious of all is to ride closer to the edge of the trail on a smooth section and, by adjusting your line from the preferred route through a section, you can slow down more effectively and will find more grip when cornering. If there is no other option than to ride through the bumps, the suspension can be adjusted to compensate for these high-frequency nuisances – you need a faster rebound and compression to deal with the stuttering effect that braking bumps create. Adjusting line choice, however, is the ultimate solution.

Rocks roll. Remain relaxed and let the bike move freely – it will grip up again.

◎ TIP

If you lock the rear wheel, release the pressure.

◎ KEY POINTS

- Grip the end of the lever using your first finger

- Feed in the brake slowly

- Feed both brakes together

- Feather the lever – squeezing the brake on and off

SKILL 2: NEUTRAL STANCE – ROLLING ALONG THE FLAT/ TRAIL WITH MOVEMENT

Before we start hitting trails we need to cover a few basics. Even a rider with years of experience can benefit from brushing up on their core skill set. I will take you through all the techniques and specific skill sets in this chapter and, with some dedication, you will be able to ride technical trail with more confidence and in a safe manner. Some of the skills you will be able to practise in your garden or local park, but the more advanced techniques will need to be practised at the bike park or out on the trails. Remember, repetition is the key, as practice makes permanent.

I will refer to the basic riding stance as your 'neutral stance' or 'centre'. This stance is sometimes referred to as the 'neutral position', 'attack position' or 'ready position'. You may have read material that talks about weight shifts – try to think of the bike as being the weight and not yourself. Imagine yourself floating along through the air and someone has attached a weight to your arms and legs (a.k.a. your bike).

Neutral stance. Stay relaxed and focus on the trail horizon. Dip the wrists and heels.

We are trying to be weightless and float along the trail with ease, articulating the limbs to absorb the trail input. When we shift weight we are not dramatically throwing ourselves off the front of the bike or trying to cower away from a trail feature by moving off the back of the bike. Instead we are making small movements around and above the bike to help influence its direction of travel. This is done in a very subtle manner and only in extreme circumstances do we need to thrust our own mass around to move the bike in a desired direction. Hopping up onto large features is one prime example where we coil up energy and release it in a dynamic fashion, by moving our body mass in such a way. For your everyday trail rider, this enormous weight shift concept only applies when they are trying to recover from a particular and often unnerving situation. Through the use of good technique, we remove the need for using brute force.

Avoid sitting down when coasting down trails. When you are seated you limit the amount of movement you have to manoeuvre the bike below you. There is a popular misconception that we move our body around over the bike, but in actual fact we are trying to move the bike around below us, keeping our head and upper body relatively still.

Hit your palm with your wrist bent at ninety degrees – think about a Kung Fu master smashing bricks. Now ask yourself where the load from the bump force is dissipated when you are riding. By lifting the brake levers up we naturally dip the wrist and gain control.

SKILL 2.1: NEUTRAL STANCE

- Pedal along at approximately jogging pace then freewheel (a slight downhill gradient will make things a little easier).

- Stop pedalling and bring your favoured foot to the front, keeping your crank arms level (parallel to the ground).

◎ DEFINITION

You will have a favoured foot that leads, which will be referred to as your lead foot. The other foot, which trails, will be referred to as your trailing foot.

- You should have the ball of your foot just slightly in front of the pedal axle.

◎ TIP

Aim to stay centred over the bike and relaxed at all times.

- Stand up on the pedals and keep your body centred on the bike, above the bottom bracket. Excessive forward weight shifts will load the front wheel and increase the potential for a forward dismount should you hit a sizable bump. Shift your weight too far off the back and you will lighten the steering and risk losing control.

- Relax, look ahead and dip slightly at the ankles, dropping your heels. You should be tall and proud above the bike but resist the temptation to lock out your limbs. The wrists should also be dipped slightly, ready to absorb any impacts.

Progress the technique

- Practise rolling along in your neutral stance, swapping your lead foot. The ability to ride with either foot leading (switch stance or ambidextrous riding) will help you with more advanced techniques.

- Lower your body through the knees, hips and arms, keeping yourself centred over the bike, moving in the vertical plane. Your weight should be transferred through the legs and feet, with minimal weight being transferred through the bars via your arms – dipping your wrists will help eliminate putting huge loads through the bars.

- You have an enormous amount of suspension available to you through your limbs and you need to remain relaxed, ready to absorb any hits through your arms and legs. There is a fine balance to find here – if you are too relaxed you will be bouncing all over the place and may be compressed into the bike on larger bumps and dips in the trail. Stay too stiff and you will pinball from hit to hit, out of control. This may take some time to perfect but be patient, it will come.

- Articulate your body to lean the bike out to your left and right while looking ahead, focused on the trail in front of you. Maintain a relaxed grip while doing so, keeping your torso reasonably upright and your head still.

- Lower your right pedal so the crank arm is vertical, or in the six o'clock position, and lean the bike over to the left.

- Repeat this by lowering the left pedal so the cranks are vertical and lean the bike to the right. Listen to the tyres as the edges cut into the surface. Return to centre.

- While rolling along in your neutral stance, try pushing the bike out in front of you. Think about your torso remaining still as you push the bike through by extending your arms (and legs from the knee down) out in front of you. To start the movement you may find it helps to move forwards slightly by just a few degrees, to coil up energy in the arms. Feel the pressure in the shoulders before you dynamically punch the bike out in front. This is the same movement that you will need to deploy in order to take large, square-edge drops or in situations where the trail fades from below you.

 TIP

Where you look, you will go.

 TIP

After every movement always return to centre, relaxed and focused.

◎ PRACTICE TIPS

- Warm-up exercise: Roll along in your neutral stance, dropping your heels and gently increasing the amount you dip the heels. Feel your calf muscles stretch, count to nine then swap your lead foot and repeat.

- Those of you using clip-in pedals may want to move your cleats back to assist with dipping the heels. Most manufacturers of specific cycling shoes have crossed over from the road-riding scene, where riders will tend to pedal with their toes pointing down. When riding mountain bikes we need to focus on riding with the heels dipped – if you ride toe down, you open up the potential of your foot to be bounced off the pedal, especially when using flat pedals. Try both styles and feel the difference for yourself.

Make sure your cleats are square on the sole and the bolts are tight.

◎ SKILL 2.2: SELECTING THE CORRECT GEAR – SHIFTING GEAR

Mountain bikes come equipped with a huge range of gears that enable us to select a ratio for pretty much every occasion. Standing up and shifting gear are critical components that help us achieve consistent quality riding. I won't bore you with technical data and talk about specific rpm (revolutions per minute) at this stage of the game, as there are so many variables in mountain biking that can affect your choice of gear. I will, however, emphasise the point that constant gear changing and finding a consistent rpm will help you get more from your ride. Riding in too small or too large a gear is inefficient and will reduce the distance that you are capable of covering.

■ Reduce the amount of tension/effort you are putting through the drive system when shifting gear.

■ Find a gear you feel comfortable in. Avoid pushing too large (heavy) a gear as this will burn excessive calories; likewise avoid spinning in too small a gear.

■ When pedalling into a climb, resist the temptation to dump down into a small gear as you hit the gradient. Instead, shift down through the gears, one at a time, when the load through the legs has increased to the point at which it is becoming more difficult to drive the pedals around.

Well-maintained drive components will last for years if they are not abused. Clean and adjust them on a regular basis.

- When descending, shift up onto the big outer chainring to help avoid chain slap. This will also cover the teeth of the outer chainring, which could act like a buzz saw should you have an accident and the bike falls on top of you.

SKILL 2.3: TRACK STANDS

You may have seen a cycle courier or road cyclist balancing at the traffic lights, waiting for that green light – we call this a 'track stand'. The name comes from the popular sport of track cycling, where riders slow to a stop and entice each other into making an attack in short sprint races. This is a great skill to learn and practise, as it helps you develop core stability and improves your balance. Trials riders are masters of this art and many of us aspire to have the bike handling skills they possess. The skill can also be useful when trail riding and often comes into play when taking on a technical climb – you can stop, balance, assess a line and then attack it.

Back in the eighties getting in and out of those wretched toe clips was a major pain. Learning the track stand helped tremendously when negotiating obstacles like a large log. If the run in and run out were limited, and we could not bunny hop the log, the sequence would start with a track stand. The bike was lined up and each wheel lifted over independently before riding out clean, all the while trying to avoid using the brakes and relying on tension and trail input.

⊚ TIP

Look for a small edge to rest your front wheel against. This will help you focus on the trail surface and will provide extra resistance.

- **Find a slight uphill gradient with a good even surface. Pedal along in your middle chainring and in about third gear on the rear, driving the pedals around slowly.**

- **Feel the tension through your legs and the gradient working against you.**

- Slow your pedal rate right down so you are barely moving.

- As your lead foot comes to the front, try to pause (your crank will be at two o'clock if you are right foot forward and at ten o'clock if you are left foot forward). Simultaneously, turn your front wheel about 45 degrees in the direction of your lead foot. The shoulders should run parallel to the handlebars; the wrists and heels should also be dipped.

Move the bike in the lateral plane by pressuring through the hands and rocking the bike left/right – move the bars, as opposed to turning the front wheel. Pressure, tension and resistance are key things to get to grips with.

Keep focusing on a spot about 1m in front of your wheel, relaxing the neck to look forwards and downwards. Stand tall and proud over the bike so the skeletal system, rather than the muscular system, supports the body's mass (think of a tightrope or slack-line walker).

◎ **TIP**

Learn to feel the trail through the four points of contact – the hands and the feet.

Drive the cranks round slowly through 360 degrees, feeling the tension in the legs and pause again.

Repeat the process, trying to pause for longer each time you stop.

Avoid snapping on the cranks by back pedalling. We need to develop a super-smooth pedal stroke using tension. Torque equals traction, and slow-speed riding is a great way to develop this skills set.

Progress the technique

- Practise the above, only this time swap out your favoured foot and try slowing to a stop with your non-favoured foot at the front.

- Pause for longer and hold the track stand.

- Challenge yourself by looking around you and engaging in a conversation.

- Take one hand off the bars.

- Try doing track stands while sitting down.

◎ TIP

Building confidence at slow speed is key and to complement this we need to practise in a safe, controlled environment. Doing so will help you ride more confidently in technical terrain at higher speeds. Not only do any bad habits we have in a slow-speed situation carry through to a high-speed situation, but also our movement from rider input is magnified significantly in a high-speed situation.

A fun experiment

- Find a low, clean log or wall.

- Stand at the end and focus on a point or a friend at 90 degrees to the log/wall. Now try to walk along to the other end.

- Repeat the process but this time focus on the end of the log/wall. See how much easier it is when we focus on where we want to be.

Concentrating the power of the mind is an important factor if you want to progress your riding. You perform many day-to-day tasks that have become second nature through repetition. The memory of the key components to perform these tasks is locked away in subconscious memory in the brain and in muscle memory. Through repetition we become familiar with tasks. Riding is a combination of key tasks/skills that are deployed instantaneously to achieve a required outcome, such as cleaning a section or whole trail. Concentration, control and commitment are key factors that help us achieve our goals and are applicable to all aspects of life, not just our trail riding.

SKILL 2.4: SLOW-SPEED RIDING – UPHILL

Slow-speed riding is a great way to iron out those bad habits. Mark out a slalom course on a mellow gradient in a safe place and ride up through the course as slowly as you can. Focus on maintaining a smooth pedal stroke and look through the turns. This sequence demonstrates looking, body position and footwork. Good pedal timing is imperative to enable you to flow through the trail continuously, pedalling in a rhythmic manner. Learn these key points at a slow speed in a safe environment before progressing on to a technical trail.

- Approach pedalling slowly spotting your line.

- Look through the turn.

- Here you can look down as the speed is low.

- As you round the turn spot for the next turn.

- Keep your pedalling smooth and consistent.

- Swing the front wheel out wide.

- Spot your line.

- Look through the turn.

- Continue to pedal through the turn and keep the brakes covered.

- Try and clip the cone with your rear wheel, challenge yourself on each run.

- Repeat the process on each turn.

- Steer by pushing the outer end of your handlebar.

- Make the course tighter as you improve.

- Practising slow speed riding improves your core stability and is a safe way to iron out bad habits and increase your confidence.

For a novice rider this is also a great way to help find the perfect gear. Ride up the course in a large gear, then on your next run try using one of your smallest gears. When we use too small a gear the tension and torque is lost; use too large a gear and you stall out in the turns. We must make lots of gear changes in an effort to keep a consistent rpm as the trail undulates.

When you have found your preferred gear, move your course markers and make the slalom more challenging – just remember to keep it slow.

SKILL 2.5: SLOW-SPEED RIDING – DOWNHILL

Using the same tight slalom course, roll back down through the turns and focus on your vision and footwork. This time we are looking to perfect braking alongside body position and footwork. Roll your cranks round in a smooth fluid motion as you make the transition between turns, remembering to have your inner pedal up at each marker and riding out wide to see through the turn to the next marker. Feed those brakes in gently, and challenge yourself by adjusting the markers to make tighter turns.

- This time focus on looking through the turn and rolling the cranks round so your inner pedal is up in the mid point of the corner.

- You may need to apply the brake to control your speed.

■ Swing out wide to you can look through the turn into the next one.

■ Roll the cranks around in a smooth fluid motion.

■ Keep your torso upright and lean the bike in, as you exit the first turn keep rolling the cranks round so you are set up for the next turn.

To steer round the tight turns, lean the bike in and push the bar with the outer hand. Resist dropping your inner elbow and pulling on the bar – keep a relaxed grip to help you.

◎ SKILL 2.6: SLOW-SPEED RIDING – CIRCLES

Standing up, pedal along at a steady walking pace in a wide turn around a marker on the floor. Progressively decrease your radius around the marker.

■ Ride along stood up towards the cone about one metre out.

■ Make a turn around the cone and tighten up the steering so you are getting closer and closer to the cone.

■ Keep looking over your shoulder at the cone as you turn tighter and tighter.

■ You will need to ride progressively slower to make a tighter turn.

■ Too much force on the cranks and the front wheel will want to wash out.

As you make a couple of turns around the marker you should be slowing your speed accordingly, to match the severity of the turn. Remember to look down over your shoulder through the turn, aiming to get the rear wheel to touch the marker. When you are very close to the marker, your bars will be at 90 degrees and you will be scrubbing the back wheel round on the spot.

Repeat the process in the reverse direction. Another good exercise that will help improve your slow-speed control and cornering is riding a simple figure of eight on a smooth flat surface. Here you can really feel the difference when you push on the handlebars as opposed to pulling on them. There are so many times on a ride when you can be playing around, practising and perfecting your technique. Slow down your riding, break it down and bag that extra practice – it's not all about getting the bike straight out of the car and blasting round the trail.

SKILL 3: LOOKING – TRAIL HORIZON

Earlier in this section we covered some basics on vision – where we look, we will go. So let's expand on that and examine how we look at the trail. As I mentioned earlier, the distance away from your wheel needs to increase as your speed increases, but it's not simply a case of looking at any one spot at any given speed. We need to train our eyes, as they are capable of tuning in to fine detail, as well as taking in information using our peripheral field of vision. This may sound complicated but let me give you some examples.

On a slow-speed climb we need to be looking at the detail of the trail, taking into consideration the need for traction, and focusing on finding the smoothest line that offers the most amount of grip. But at the same time, we have to try to predict and be looking at where the trail goes. We use our peripheral vision to keep an eye on the hill line and to look for obstacles that may require an adjustment in technique and therefore body

position. For instance, you may spot in the distance something like a tight switchback, a continuation of the gradient or a technical obstacle like a rock-up step (a step-up).

The technique is the same whether travelling on the flat or descending – it's just a simple case of you having to respond faster if descending. At this point I have to emphasise again the importance of starting slow then building up speed.

To look at it in more detail, let's consider the processes that a trials rider goes through when hopping up and over multiple obstacles. They have already assessed and planned their route even before they have got on their bike. They know in their 'mind's eye' exactly where their wheel needs to be to clear the obstacle. Through practice they have learned to understand exactly what shapes they must make to get the bike to respond accordingly, to the extent that they can place their wheel within a square inch. As they start their first move, they are spotting for the exact spot to land their wheel. In this scenario there is less need for them to use their peripheral vision as they have already predetermined their line. They will of course, on occasion, look up and around to complete the image they have created in their mind during their assessment of the obstacle/section.

For most of you reading this, you will probably just want to ride a trail and get a little bit more enjoyment from it. One of the things that makes riding so fulfilling for me is the sense of achievement gained from cleaning a technical section or riding a whole trail in a smooth and fluid fashion. Visualisation is a key skill that enables us to achieve this.

■ **Avoid looking down directly in front of you.**

■ **As the speed increases look further down the trail.**

■ **Always look to the furthest point on the trail.**

Getting to know a trail is imperative but that is not to say we shouldn't hone our skills to enable us to ride blind trails and still achieve our goals. To do this we need to practise and be able to visualise where we want to be on the trail at any given time. When top riders talk about and look at line choice, they are honing their vision, taking in all the detail around them and creating an imaginary line where they want their wheels to be. All the other information – for example, there is a large stump to the left of my line and a rock over there – becomes redundant.

Just take a basic section of trail and we can highlight many details: roots, rocks and earth, or 'RRE'. There may be other factors to consider but let's keep it to these simple three. Considering the average tyre is two inches wide, we can safely say we have 18 possible lines through a piece of trail that is three feet wide. All we need to do, and simple as it may sound, is select our two-inch wide strip and commit to it. Staying focused – and using correct technique, body position, footwork and speed control – we can ride the most technically demanding trails.

Think about a racing game on your games console. At first you have to drive slower cars that unlock the faster cars for you to drive at a later stage, once you have gained experience. Or putting it another way, you wouldn't go from driving your family saloon to jumping straight into a Formula One racing car. The brain has to get up to speed and it's through direct experience that we can achieve this.

SKILL 4: FOOTWORK – CORNERING

Ever find you are drifting wide on the exit of corners? Or maybe you exit a turn thinking that you could have gone faster through it? Personally, I would rather say the latter, as carrying too much speed into a corner can end in an unfavourable situation. A wise man once told me: 'Slow in, quick out'. Speed control, body position and footwork are the key components of mastering corners. We have to control our speed, preferably in a straight line, as we enter the corner, rather than using the brakes mid-turn, which will cause us to slide. Remember, torque equals traction, and if we can pedal through a turn or on the exit of it, we can therefore corner faster and safer.

SKILL 4.1: SLOW-SPEED CORNER

You will find when climbing there is no option but to pedal through the turn. On the odd occasion there may be RRE that you have to negotiate – simply change your footwork accordingly, to avoid smashing the pedals into the earth.

◎ **DEFINITION**

RRE – roots, rocks and earth.

◎ **TIP**

By developing your footwork and learning to ride 'switch stance' (also referred to as switch foot) you can corner faster and with more confidence. This technique changes your body position so your hips are pointing into the corner.

As you approach the turn, spot for the smoothest line and look through the turn to see if it tightens up, the gradient gets steeper or the trail levels out. Simultaneously, as you approach the turn preselect your gear accordingly.

- **Control your speed as you approach the turn in your neutral stance. Look at where the trail heads on the exit of the turn.**

- **Select your gear and adjust your speed and footwork while spotting your line.**

- **Remain relaxed and focused.**

- Remember for a right hand turn approach with your left leg leading.

- Keep as wide as possible on the entry allowing you to take a smooth radius through the turn.

- Look for RRE in the turn.

- Drive the cranks around as you take the corner, in the photo sequence you can see a small wheelie has been added to clear loose rocks.

- By matching the front wheel on to the upper trail, the risk of the front end washing out has been removed.

- As you exit the turn on your desired line drive the pedals round and climb out.

- Ride out clean.

Steer round the turn and continue to look through it, pushing on the handlebars rather than pulling. On a right turn, drive through with the left arm and resist pulling with the right one – when we pull on the inside of a turn, it tends to tuck the front wheel under you.

FLAT CORNERS

I just want to eliminate another old myth at this point. Now, I think the following problem has occurred due to the translation of the information rather than its content. The old way of thinking was that we rode turns with our inner pedal up and our outer pedal down. Physics will once again put paid to this notion. For sure, at some point in a turn we need our

TIP

Remember, at higher speeds, turn by leaning the bike and not by turning the handlebars. Avoid dropping your inner elbow as this will make the bike tuck under you.

pedals/cranks in this position, but the critical issue is, when? Learning to plant your outer crank at the right time will dramatically increase the grip and control you have in the turn.

The old theory comes from road cycling, where there are five points of contact – two hands on the bars, two feet on the pedals, and then there's your bottom planted on the seat. Because you are seated, an element of load is transferred through the bike, via the seat and seat tube, as well as to the crank area. However, when we stand up on a mountain bike, this fifth point is missing and we no longer transfer weight from the torso through the bottom. We are putting a larger percentage of weight through our feet and the cranks. As we can move more independently from the bike we can and need to adjust our technique in the turns. This is our saving grace on slippery surfaces, as below us the bike has an element of freedom to squirm around.

So let's look at the mechanics here. If we approach a left-hand turn and drop our right foot in anticipation, where does the majority of the load go? Through the right leg/pedal and crank. Try this with your bike standing in front of you and see which way the bike leans – as you will see this makes the bike lean to the right. Now, which way does our turn go? We are leaning the bike the wrong way for the turn using this antiquated technique. For this reason we ride into the initial part of the turn with cranks level. Our weight is more evenly distributed and we can lean the bike into the turn, after which we start to lower the outer pedal. This lowering will happen through the turn and this is a critical point – by developing this style and getting the timing correct you can corner faster, harder and safer.

The larger piece of stone rolled as the rear wheel crossed it causing the back end to slip out, the other smaller stones then break away as the wheel skips over the surface. Stay relaxed, breathe, no problem.

◎ FACT

Q. What is the next thing to happen when a wheel starts to slide out?

A. It begins to grip again.

To increase the grip further, you can roll your foot inside your shoe as if you were putting a ski on edge to turn. We can influence the bike's movement a huge amount with foot rolling – for instance, when a wheelie starts to veer off to one side we can correct it by rolling the foot on the pedal. Learning to steer with your feet really opens up your riding.

I cannot emphasise enough how important it is to stay relaxed at all times. Should your wheel start to slide, it will eventually find something to grip upon again – even the smallest lip will offer support, if only for an instant. Learn to trust your tyres and you will find riding and sliding go hand in hand. Top racers use drift to corner faster, but that is an advanced skill and requires a lot of dedication and commitment.

⊚ SKILL 4.2: FLAT CORNERS – SHALLOW RADIUS

Shallow radius – left turn

- Approach the turn in your neutral stance, with your right foot forward. This will enable you to recover from a situation, e.g. sliding out.

- Look through the corner for RRE.

- Select your line.

- Adjust your speed accordingly.

- Spot your exit.

- Stay focused.

- Lean the bike into the turn.

- Keep the wrists and heels dipped.

- Remember to lean the bike over, keeping your torso vertical.

- Keep your head still but remain relaxed in the neck and shoulders.

- Stay focused on your exit point, hit it and ride out clean.

Shallow radius – right turn

- Same procedure as for the left turn, except now approach the turn with your left foot forward.

◎ SKILL 4.3: FLAT CORNERS – MEDIUM RADIUS

Medium radius – left turn

- Approach the turn in your neutral stance, with your right foot forward (this is where the importance of learning how to ride switch stance comes into play).

- Look through the corner for RRE.

- Select your line.

- Adjust your speed accordingly.

- Spot your exit.

- Stay focused.

- Lean the bike into the turn.

- Keep the wrists and heels dipped.

- Remember to lean the bike over, keeping your torso vertical.

- Keep your head still but remain relaxed in the neck and shoulders.

- As we progress through the turn we slowly roll the cranks round and aim to have our outer (right) foot planted (right crank at six o'clock) at a point approximately two-thirds of the way through the turn (the apex point).

- Continue with the smooth pedal stroke and drive the cranks round as you exit the turn.

Medium radius – right turn

- Same procedure as for the left turn, except now approach the turn with your left foot forward.

SKILL 4.4: FLAT CORNERS – TIGHT RADIUS

Tight radius – right turn

- Approach the turn in your neutral stance, with your left foot forward (this is where the importance of learning how to ride switch stance comes into play).

- Look through the corner for RRE.

- Select your line.

- Adjust your speed accordingly.

- Spot your exit.

- Stay focused.

- Lean the bike into the turn.

- Keep the wrists and heels dipped.

- Remember to lean the bike over, keeping your torso vertical.

- Keep your head still but remain relaxed in the neck and shoulders.

- As we progress through the turn we slowly roll the cranks round and aim to have our outer (right) foot planted (right crank at six o'clock) at a point approximately three-quarters of the way through the turn (the apex point).

- Continue with the smooth pedal stroke and drive the cranks round as you exit the turn.

Tight radius – left turn

Approach the turn in your neutral stance, with your right foot forward.

Multiple corners will mean multiple adjustments to footwork, body position and speed control.

- You never know what nature will throw at you and drops between turns or mid-turn make you work harder.

- By taking the drop over the rock the rider is able to take a wider line in the final tight turn, it also enables him to see round the bush and spot his exit line.

- The wider line in the final turn will also help to avoid loose rocks.

Progress the technique

- Roll your foot inside your shoe to increase the load on the inner edge of the outer pedal (where pedal attaches to crank arm). This small rotation, done in synchronisation with the outer foot being lowered, increases the grip by a huge amount.

- Find a mellow gradient on smooth grass or on a closed road (grass is preferable due to its forgiving nature).

- Mark up a simple slalom course, using cones, sticks or spare clothing (you need to be able to roll over the marker should you get the line wrong).

- Freewheel through the course without pedalling through the turns, but remember to roll the cranks over and get your footwork dialled. Develop your own language and get a friend to help by calling 'inner up' or 'outer down' – whatever works best for you.

- Tighten up the course and change the gates around so each turn requires a different approach.

- Slalom practice is a great way to perfect speed control and footwork.

- Start slow and build your speed up.

- Aim to coast through the course without braking.

- Run your internal dialogue and rail those turns.

- Roll the foot in the shoe to increase traction.

- Ride out clean and head up for another run.

BERMED/BANKED TURNS

Many purpose-built trails feature bermed corners. Unfortunately there are no hard and fast rules to these types of turn, as each trail is built and weathers differently. Some corners may be washed out and the banking simply disappears part-way round; others could be steeper or more shallow. Here are some key things to consider when riding berms.

- Apply the same technique that is used for flat corners. On bermed turns with a shallow radius, you will be able to ride the section with your cranks level.

- Momentum is your friend and you will have to commit to the turn in order for the forces to help you stick to the trail. Ride too slowly and you will slip towards the bottom of the turn.

- Try to choose the smoothest line around the turn and set your course as you enter the turn.

- Avoid riding at the top of the berm as it may be blown out further round or on the exit.

- Avoid riding on the loose earth down on the inside of the turn.

- Turn by leaning the bike, keeping your torso upright.

- Stay relaxed, looking through the turn to spot your exit.

- Ride out clean.

We can also roll the crank around in bermed turns and this process can help us get more grip. As you reach the deepest point of the turn, drop your outer foot and roll the foot in the shoe. Continue in one smooth action to drive the cranks round as you begin to exit the turn. Spotting your exit, pedal out of the corner and set up for the next feature.

SKILL 5: OFF-CAMBER AND OFF-CAMBER TURNS

When riding steep gradients on natural terrain you may come across off-camber sections that need to be traversed. They will of course have the inevitable corner or two thrown in for good measure. Here are some pointers to help you deal with such sections.

- Look for supporting edges to cross the hill. There may be a worn line but if not, spot for RRE to support you (even a lip half-inch high will suffice).

- Increase the pressure in the heels and if the terrain is very steep, position your cranks so that the pedal on the downside is at the bottom. This will help with ground clearance and allow you to lean further into the hill.

- As you approach a turn control your speed. You will need a much slower entry speed into turns, as the gradient you are about to drop into will add pace.

- Try to stay high and wide into turns.

- Spot your exit.

- Stay focused.

- Lean the bike into the turn.

- Keep the wrists and heels dipped.

- Remember to lean the bike over, keeping your torso vertical.

- Keep your head still but remain relaxed in the neck and shoulders.

- Look for lips to support you on the exit – even things like the base of a tree can be used to hook upon.

- Spot your exit and ride out clean.

Off camber turns can be tricky.

SKILL 6: WHEELIES

There are two ways in which we can pick up the front end of the bike. The first method I will look at requires synchronising a pedal stroke while scooping under the handlebars to lift the front wheel in the air. This technique is deployed when taking a drop at super-slow speed or clearing a trail feature like a step-up when climbing. It is also a whole load of fun riding around on the rear wheel and, as you will see, it is essential practice if you wish to hold sustained manuals. To start with, we just need to get the timing down and clear small obstacles, but the real fun begins when we perfect the technique and can float along on the neutral balance point on the rear wheel.

Timing is the key and you will find a larger percentage of lift comes from driving the crank round, not by pulling on the handlebars. Think about scooping from underneath the bars and you will find you get more lift with less effort. This is a key thing to perfect as the manual lift requires this action in order to get lift without the use of pedalling. By performing and perfecting proper wheelies, we get used to the neutral balance point on the rear wheel and, hopefully, eliminate the fear of looping out.

◎ TIP

I highly recommend using flat pedals. You will be able to step clear from the bike if it all gets a little too much.

- Find a slight uphill gradient on a smooth surface, with lots of space around you – short grass is the preferred choice thanks to its forgiving nature.

- Select a low gear but stay in your middle chainring (middle ring and gear four on the rear).

- Pedal along at a steady walking pace.

- Cover the rear brake to prevent looping out should you lift beyond the neutral pivot point.

- As your lead foot comes round to twelve o'clock, dip your torso forwards, pivoting through the hips and bending at the elbows.

- Just as the crank passes one o'clock for a right foot lead (or eleven o'clock for a left foot lead), dynamically increase the load/pedal rate while simultaneously scooping under the bar and moving your torso backwards, pivoting from the hips. As the torso moves back, the arms will extend and lock out at the elbow (pop and lock – 'pop up' pivoting through the hips from our dipped elbows using the lower back, and 'lock' the extended arms out). Keep your bottom planted in the seat and imagine you are trying to drive the rear wheel underneath you – it also helps to keep the chin up a little. This is all done in one smooth, fluid motion.

- Continue to drive the cranks round.

- This is where the lift really comes from. At this point a dynamic pedal stroke lifts the front end.

- Practise on different gradients and using different gears.

- Practise starting a wheelie using your non-favoured foot.

You will find there is a neutral balance point where you will neither loop out nor drop the front wheel.

As you drive the cranks round keep monitoring the back brake and apply a little pressure if necessary. Hopefully you have perfected the art of smooth braking as it really comes into play when sustaining wheelies. If your wheelie drops off and you find you are increasing your pedal rate and spinning through the gear, then you have not lifted the front wheel high enough with your initial effort/pedal stroke. To give you some idea, the front wheel should reach its maximum/optimum height within one-third of a pedal stroke.

Progress the technique

- Start by lifting your front wheel over a small stick or a line marked on the floor.

- Mark a line to start a wheelie and see how far you can go.

- Practise placing your wheel down on a specific point/spot on the floor.

- Practise by using your non-favoured foot to take off from – this is a 'switch wheelie' and a great skill to perfect, as you never know when and where you need to pop a wheelie.

- Ride down the gradient and, once up in the wheelie, stop pedalling and try to coast along. This is a great way to get into manuals. You will have to drive the bike below you by dipping the heels and standing up, out of the saddle. Extend through the knees and keep your weight right off the back – it helps if your saddle is slightly lower than your normal cross-country ride height.

◎ **TIP**

If you are going to loop out the following two points will help return your front wheel to terra firma.

- Gently blend in the rear brake.
- Lower your chest towards the stem by dipping down and bending at the elbows.

◎ **TIP**

You may just not have your crank positioned with your favoured foot at the front when you need it, so you should practise switch wheelies.

All the work is done in the initial snap. The height to which you lift your wheel during the start of the sequence is the limiting factor as to whether you continue to wheelie or the front wheel drops back to the floor.

- To progress on to coasting first pop up into a wheelie.

- Gather a little pace when you are up.

- Stop pedalling with your cranks at three o'clock (or nine o'clock for a left foot lead). Stand up by extending out from the knee. Dip the heels.

- Cover the rear brake and coast along.

When you get really good, you will be able to put turns into your wheelies by leaning the bike over, left or right.

SKILL 7: PUMPING

Pumping is a key component of your riding CV – when we articulate our body in time with the motion of the bike and terrain, we flow through the trail in a seemingly effortless manner. When we are relaxed and supple, yet strong, we can manage our mass with ease and gain every ounce of momentum from the trail. When we tense up, stop breathing and dip our chin we start to get out of rhythm with the trail and things become unpleasant. Mountain biking is an art form – think of it as a martial art. If we take a look at Shaolin monks, they are not overbuilt gym warriors, yet they are considered to be super strong. True strength comes from tendons and not from muscles. Shaolin monks are masters at switching between soft-and-supple mode and strong-like-steel mode – we can learn a lot from this and apply it to our riding.

When we pump through a trail and gain free energy, we simply turn the dials from being rooted heavy and planted in the dips to being light and airy as we crest the humps, bumps and whoops. The process of changing modes happens at a rapid rate. We need to be supple and soft and able to switch the dials when huge strength is required to bring the bike back into line, or to squash out a feature absorbing its energy up into our body.

All whoops and humps are different but the technique is the same. Single pump bumps can be taken on either by squashing them out and floating out the lip with a manual down the far side slope, or by doing a manual before the bump and planting your front wheel down on the far side. When you have multiple pump bumps or whoops then you need to squash them out or where possible jump the lot.

- Approach in your neutral stance. Look ahead through the section.

- Press down as you go through the bottom of the whoop, use the suspension in your arms and legs to soak up the bump as you hit the slope.

- As your front wheel crests the bump move up in to the front centre so your navel is in line on the vertical with your bottom bracket axle.

- From this extended position lift the bike up and over the bumps by sucking it up into the body. Your limbs do the work for you acting as natural suspension.

- Repeat the process as you crest and dip through the whoops, pressuring out in the bottom and going heavy to lift up and going light over the crest.

- Keep centred on the bike as you push it down and away from you.

- Practice makes permanent.

SKILL 8: MANUALS

The manual is a very useful skill and an essential one if you aim to cruise through trails with ease. By lifting our front wheel over trail features, we eliminate a high percentage of resistance from those that impede our momentum in the forward plane. Everything that opposes us, from small upslopes to square-edge rocks and nasty roots, can be manualled over. Once the front half of the bike is over the feature, our rear wheel just rattles along behind us like a trailer, with our mass aiding it in the process. The manual is a key skill that helps us pump through the trail, making us more efficient, and also helps to eliminate the potential for being jacked up or thrusted into the front of the bike.

◎ TIP

Use flat pedals and you'll be able to step clear from the bike if it all gets a little too much.

- Find a slight downhill gradient on a smooth surface with lots of space around you – short grass is the preferred choice thanks to its forgiving nature.

- Roll along at a steady jogging pace in your neutral stance.

- Cover the rear brake to prevent looping out should you lift beyond the neutral pivot point. The same is applicable here as for the wheelie – you can lower the front wheel by dipping the elbows, bringing the chest closer to the stem.

- Move forwards by bending the elbows and pivoting through the hips, dipping at the knees slightly as you do so.

- As you accelerate up and away from the bike moving towards the rear, simultaneously scoop the bar from underneath while driving the heels down (when you push into the pedals you may find dipping the toes helps you get more lift). Drive the bike underneath you by dipping the heels and extending the legs, this is all done in one smooth fluid motion.

TIP

I cannot emphasise enough how much difference it makes when you scoop under the bar. Not only is the initial lift easier but you can also hold the weight for longer. To help sustain the manual you may find it easier to lower your seat. Those of you riding cross-country trails will find it harder to sustain the manual with the seat at the normal ride height – the area you have to move your hips in is the exact spot where your seat lies.

The manual is one of the hardest skills to write a clear description of; it is something that you have to learn to feel, and practice is essential if you wish to perfect it.

Progress the technique

- Start by lifting your front wheel over a small stick or a line marked on the floor.

- Mark a line from which to start a manual and see how far you can coast with the front wheel in the air. Want to go further? Simply go faster.

- Practise placing your wheel down on a specific point/spot on the floor.

- Practise by using your non-favoured foot from which to start the manual – this is a 'switch manual' and a great skill to perfect, as you never know when and where you need to pop a manual.

- Bringing timing into the skill is essential, as matching features and blending the wheels in to the terrain is all about timing. Bringing visual cues to any skill will help you master it and bury the message deep in your subconscious.

SKILL 9: THE BUNNY HOP

Now you have perfected the manual you have the opening move to do a bunny hop, which is a very useful tool at it enables us to clear obstacles on the trail and pre-jump into down slopes. The shapes you make in the bunny hop are the same ones you make when jumping, so to jump safely it is essential to perfect your hops. The correct technique used for hopping involves lifting your two wheels independently and not together as some people think.

Some cross-country riders have developed a bad technique of cheating the lift by pulling up with their feet using the clip-in pedals. The other dangerous technique I have seen is bouncing the bike to facilitate a similar two-wheeled lift. This method is dangerous as your bike becomes a dead weight hanging from your limbs. You lose the ability to move and place the bike where required and you have to hop much further for both wheels to clear an obstacle.

With the correct technique of lifting the front wheel using a manual, then hopping (lifting) the rear wheel over, we save energy and can move the bike left and right in the process. Our rear wheel only has to travel a short distance to clear the obstacle and is no longer airborne for very long. To enable you to pull a lateral, or sideways, hop you will need to articulate (pivot) on your rear wheel (*see* Skill 10). This is a great skill to bag as it enables you to recover from an undesired line choice – deep grooves in mud (ruts) from a vehicle are one prime example where this skill pays dividends.

Once again it is important to learn good technique and I recommend you use flat pedals while practising the skill.

◎ TIP

A bunny hop is basically a manual with a snap and a lift.

- Find a slight downhill gradient on a smooth surface with lots of space around you – short grass is the preferred choice thanks to its forgiving nature.

- Roll along at a steady jogging pace in your neutral stance.

- Cover the rear brake to prevent looping out should you lift beyond the neutral pivot point. The same is

applicable here as for the wheelie – you can lower the front wheel by dipping the elbows, bringing the chest closer to the stem.

- Move forwards by bending the elbows and pivoting through the hips, dipping at the knees slightly as you do so.

- As you accelerate up and away from the bars, extending the arms, scoop the bar from underneath while dipping the heels.

- Drive the bike underneath you by extending your legs back out so they are close to being locked out. Think about driving the bike out in front of you.

- The height of your hop will be limited to the height you can achieve in this initial lift.

- As the front wheel reaches its optimum height, lift the bars upwards and drive them up and away from you, simultaneously springing up from your dipped heels. This is the snap point where you need to move in a fast, dynamic style. Your trailing foot will naturally point toe down and you need to apply pressure back against the pedal to help the lift.

- Lift your legs up into the torso, spot your landing and place the bike back down gently, with the rear wheel contacting just before the front one.

- Ride out clean.

Progress the technique

- Bring timing into the skill by placing a marker on the floor to hop from/over.

- Place a small stick/log on the floor to hop over. Make sure it is free from debris and will roll should you accidentally land on it.

- Practise placing your wheel down on a specific point/spot on the floor.

- Practise by using your non-favoured foot to start the hop from – this is a 'switch bunny hop' and a great skill to perfect as you never know when and where you need to pop a bunny hop.

◎ **TIP**

Think about the right hand end of the handlebars making a number-five shape.

◎**TIP**

Consider conserving energy by only hopping a minimal amount – there is no point hopping 1m in the air to clear an obstacle that is 10cm high.

SKILL 10: THE LATERAL BUNNY HOP

TO THE RIGHT

■ As you roll into the manoeuvre make a slight turn to the right. This should be done at the same time as you start the manual.

■ As you approach, focus on your line over the feature.

■ Adjust your speed and footwork.

■ Turn into the direction you want to hop leaning the bike.

■ As your front wheel moves up and across the feature, make your snap.

■ Hop up.

- Kick across with your feet to the right to get the back end to move across. Think about kicking your left leg across in an upward, scooping motion.

- Place the bike back down gently, with the rear wheel contacting just before the front.

- Ride out clean.

TO THE LEFT

- As you roll into the manoeuvre make a slight turn to the left. This should be done at the same time as you start the manual.

- As the manual reaches its peak, turn slightly to the right while making the snap and lift the rear wheel.

- Kick across with your feet to the left to get the back end to move across. Think about kicking your right leg across in an upward, scooping motion.

- Place the bike back down gently, with the rear wheel contacting just before the front.

Progress the technique

- Bring timing into the skill by placing a marker on the floor to hop from/over.

- Place a small stick/log on the floor to hop over.

- Practise placing your wheel down on a specific point/spot on the floor.

- Practise by using your non-favoured foot to start the hop from – this is a 'switch lateral bunny hop' and is a great skill to perfect as you never know when and where you need to pop a lateral bunny hop.

SKILL 11: DROP-OFFS

Like all trail features you will find many different types of drop-off, but fortunately you will only need to adjust your core technique slightly to conquer anything from a kerb to a monster shore drop. Practice makes permanent and, as with all skills, start small and build your confidence while gradually gaining height and distance.

Speed control is the key here, and mastering the ability to measure pace so it suits the angles and distances will come with time. This is where repeatedly riding a trail feature will pay dividends – through repetition you will build up memory in your subconscious to draw from in future trail situations. You will also gain all-important muscle memory so your body moves accordingly to the visual cues as well as those from the trail input.

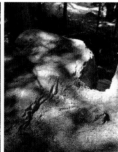

Before attempting any drop-off, you should first take a good look at the approach, the drop and the run out. This is referred to as the 'entry/section/exit' (ESE). As always – be sensible, choose a safe place to practise and be aware of other trail users. If in an urban environment, obey the rules of the road and look out for pedestrians and other road users.

◎ DEFINITION

ESE – entry/section/exit

SLOW-SPEED DROP-OFF

When the combination of a tight entry and exit prevails, you will need to perform a slow-speed drop. Other trail conditions, such as gradient and RRE, will also be factors that could turn a trail feature into a sweet spot or a hiker bike mission.

- Approach in your neutral stance, spotting the lip and exit line.

- Adjust your speed and footwork accordingly.

- Perform a wheelie just as your front wheel arrives at the lip. When you have a good, controlled wheelie you can pick up the front wheel as and when you like.

- Ride over and off the lip, preferably coasting rather than pedalling (demonstrated in the wheelie section). However, you may, depending on your speed, need to pedal through the lip with the rear wheel driving you forwards to clear RRE.

- Land rear wheel first, covering the rear brake and absorbing the landing using the ankles, knees and hips as extra suspension. Once the rear wheel has contacted, control the front wheel and place it where required while simultaneously releasing the rear brake slowly, or as fast as is necessary, according to the gradient.

- Absorb the front wheel impact through the upper body. You will have to work harder on larger drops to keep your head still and away from impacting on the stem/bars.

- Return to your neutral stance and ride out clean.

AT HIGHER SPEEDS

- Having looked at the ESE, take a suitably long run. You may want to put a little extra distance in so you can settle into your neutral stance before the drop. Stay relaxed and focused on the lip, with heels and wrists dipped.

- As you approach the lip, spot for your landing.

- Float off the lip and punch the bike out in front of you, driving through from the wrists and scooping the bars from underneath rather than pulling up on them. Your lead foot should be making the same shape, dipping at the heel and driving through, while your trailing foot will remain level, with the toe maybe dipping a little and pressuring back on the pedal gently.

- Return to centre over the bike as you free fall.

- Place the bike down by extending your limbs just before touch down.

- As the bike contacts the floor rear wheel first, begin to absorb the landing through the limbs. Remain focused, with your head still looking at your exit line and into the next section, and poised ready to make any adjustments.

- Try to match the gradient when landing into down slopes. Tighter-geometry bikes prefer to be placed down rear wheel first, but on longer-travel all-mountain and downhill bikes you can land both wheels at the same time and let your suspension do some of the work.

- Touch down. Having absorbed the landing, you will be fully compressed on large drops. Focus ahead on your exit line while returning to centre. Stay relaxed and ride out clean.

Progress the technique

■ When you have a huge hang time you can put that bit of artistic flair into your drops. More hang time means larger, slower tricks can be performed.

■ To lean the bike left, turn the bars to the right slightly while simultaneously rolling your feet on the pedals to their left edges. To enhance the movement, kick your legs across and up underneath your torso.

■ Slow drops: Mark a spot on the floor and land your rear wheel on it/ over it.

■ Remember, wheelies are another key component to mastering slow drops – manuals will help with the faster ones. Both of these can be practised pretty much anywhere you ride between extreme gradients.

■ Mental practice: Stand on your invisible bike and close your eyes. Step into the neutral stance – you're riding towards the drop – imagine there is a bar at waist height directly above the lip – it stops you and folds you over it, just before the front wheel gets air. Your arms and legs stretch out in front of you as the weight of the bike stretches you around the bar. The bar breaks and you can pull yourself back up to centre, catching up with the bike. Plant the bike on the floor, squatting to absorb the landing and ride out.

SKILL 12: JUMPS

An aspirational skill that is the golden ticket for all mountain bikers, jumping changes forever the way you look at and ride a trail. Mastering jumps enables you to ride faster and safer and have a whole load more fun in the process. When we are in the air, we are safe. Nothing can grab at your wheel and there is nothing there to make your wheel slip out – those roots just disappear as you glide past them in the air.

Jumping may seem daunting but it is actually a very easy process. We need to have perfected the manual and the bunny hop in order to jump – the shapes we make and the techniques we use are exactly the same as those performed in the bunny hop. When we have mastered feeling the terrain below our wheels and perfected the element of speed control, we can finally turn all the dials to light and soar for the sky.

When we have a lip to launch from it's a simple case of bunny hopping out of it. Longer, steeper, built and natural takeoffs require less lift and we simply let momentum do the work and make small inputs to manage the shape our bodies and bikes make. Ultimately, you will have to work a transition float through the air, line it up and absorb the landing.

Where a trail fades away we can pre-jump into the downslope by popping a bunny hop before the lip. Jumping and hopping are very useful tools that enable us to flatten out a trail. Break down the trail into sections and see where you can put a hop or a jump in to smooth it out. Remember, these skills enable us to gain momentum through a trail, saving energy. Always try to match features and use gravity from downslopes to propel you forwards with increased velocity – avoid at all costs flat landings and coming short on a feature. Speed control is essential and it will come as you spend more time riding and practising.

◎ NOTE

Smaller jumps are actually harder to clean smoothly, compared to larger ones. Unfortunately there is a misunderstanding that large features equal large accidents – this is simply not the case. There needs to be a compatibility between the proportions of your bike and the radii used to create a jump. Broken down, a jump consists of a transition onto a flat section, then either a square edge or a lip that can be measured as a radius. Your bike has wheels of a measurable diameter and a wheelbase that needs to pass over the edge or lip at a certain speed in order to clear the flat top (or gap in a double jump), and with both wheels parallel to the ground match a downslope of measurable length and final transition.

Small jumps have tight transitions that buck the bike if taken at speed – their short upslopes do not allow for a full wheelbase to sit on them before the bike is shot into the air by the final lip/radius. This causes problems for inexperienced riders as they tend to carry too much speed into small jumps (raising the question of where to put them in purpose-built trails) and struggle to squash them out. Jump them too fast at your peril, as your speed is too great to match the downslope, so a flat landing is inevitable and unsavoury.

At speed you have to work super hard to deal with kicks from oversized bumps and badly built jumps. Just close your eyes and visualise a close-up of your wheel hitting a tight, large bump at speed, then think about that same close-up of wheel and tyre rolling through a long, smooth radius takeoff. Larger features allow the bike to settle and give you more time to respond to the feeling of the ground/trail – the whole process is more relaxed even though the features are larger. Only features of this scale should be classed as jumps. Other air time comes from bump jumping – the forces that come from these large bumps is too great for the bike to simply roll over. It's the hit that propels the bike into the air and you have to respond super fast by sucking the bike up into your body and pressing it back to earth using the best suspension units you have – your limbs.

Before taking on a jump have a good look at it – consider its run-up, transition and exit. Start small and work your way up to larger, longer jumps. BMX tracks are great places to perfect jumping.

- Approach the transition in your neutral stance, leaning slightly into the front centre. Remain focused on the lip and landing zone.

- Control your speed well before you meet the transition.

- Time your opening manual moves as you flow through the start of the transition and/or up the takeoff on the upslope.

- Your body needs to move instinctively as the shape of the trail changes below you and you move through the transition onto the upslope.

- Continue lifting up, scooping under the bars as you exit the lip. Just before your rear wheel leaves the lip you are standing in the vertical position, ready to lift the bike up into your torso.

- When fully airborne, spot your landing and feed the bike up into the body, legs retracting in to the torso, and move the bike through your thighs in front of you. When you hit larger jumps and have more hang time, you can start to add a little flair to your jumps.

- As you clear the lip on the far side, nose the bike slightly so as to match the downslope. If you were hitting a bump jump, you need to keep the bike level in order to match the lesser gradient.

- Your rear wheel should be fully over the lip and the bike matched to the angle of the trail.

- Remain focused on your line as you absorb the landing through the limbs.

- Pump the transition at the bottom of the downslope as you return to centre and ride out clean.

SKILL 13: SWITCHBACKS

There are a huge variety of tight turns out there that 'switch back' on themselves and, when taking them, there are a multitude of things to consider. You will often find that the steeper the terrain, the tighter the switch (radius). In this case the trail is usually narrower and so your speed will need to be adjusted accordingly.

OPEN SWITCHBACKS (WIDER LONGER RADIUS)

- You will need to adjust your line depending on the terrain. If it is not possible to ride the outside line due to irrelevant features or 'white noise', approach on the outside edge of the trail, as far over as the terrain will allow.

- Enter the switchback, with your cranks level in the neutral stance. Remember to have your footwork dialled for maximum grip – a left switch needs to be approached with your right foot leading and vice versa. Keep the heels and wrists dipped, controlling your speed in a straight line using as much front brake as possible. Remember to stay relaxed and do your braking early. Try to avoid locking the rear wheel as this will reduce your stopping power and erode the trail.

- Look down to the trail below, spotting for rocks and roots and preselecting your line on the exit.

- Enter by swinging wide, using the bank where possible or riding as wide as the trail will allow. Carve up the bank while looking through the turn or, if there is no bank to use, stay out wide and look through the turn to the trail horizon.

- Cut down off the bank, aiming for an apex about three-quarters of the way round the inside radius. When you hit the mid-point of the turn, drop your outer foot so the cranks are in the vertical position. Continue to look through the turn, steering by pushing through with the outer hand while pressing down through the pedals.

- Resist dropping your inner elbow as this will tuck the bike in under you mid-turn. Roll the cranks round in a fluid motion through the remaining 90 degrees back to level as you complete the last part of the turn. This will set you up for the next switch or simply allow you to pedal out of the turn down the straight.

- Remember to look for RRE to support you as you make the turn.

TIGHT SWITCHBACKS – METHOD 1

- Control your speed on the entry to the switchback as in the previous section, spotting your exit line as you approach.

- Follow the same points as the open switchback – think footwork/speed control and look for your exit.

- Slow to a near stop, looking into the turn.

- Gently let off the brakes and simultaneously make a weight shift off the back of the bike, towards the inside of the turn.

- Keep your cranks level and heels dipped.

- Push through with your outer hand and continue looking through the turn.

- Avoid any RRE that may impede your momentum and try not to snatch at the brakes as this will pitch you up or skid the rear wheel.

- On super-tight, steep switchbacks you will practically pivot on the rear wheel.

- As you exit the turn make a weight shift so you return to centre for maximum braking efficiency.

- You may need to repeat the process for the next switch.

TIGHT SWITCHBACKS – METHOD 2

To master this technique you will first have to perfect Skill 14 (the endo) on page 193.

- Control your speed on the entry to the switchback as in the previous section, only this time you will need a little momentum as you enter the turn. Spot your exit line as you approach.

- From your dipped heels, spring up and simultaneously apply more front brake while starting to turn in.

- Coast into the turn on your front wheel and kick the bike round with your feet, pushing from the inside foot.

- When the bike is approximately 90 degrees to the turn, release the front brake slightly and roll down the gradient while still turning in and kicking the heels across.

- Push down with your feet, planting the rear wheel on the ground, and roll out.

This method is much faster but does come with an associated risk factor. Get it wrong and the large exposure in such terrain could bite pretty hard. When encountering multiple corners using these two techniques, you will have to readjust your footwork when exiting the turn in order to be set up for the next switch. Remember, you should always perfect your technique in a safe, controlled environment before putting your new-found skills into practice out on the trail. Sections of tight switchbacks are often out in the wilderness and miles from communications and assistance. Replicate the scenario in a safer place first, such as your local park.

◎ PRACTICE TIPS – TIGHT SWITCHBACKS

Find a slight downhill gradient. Place a cone or a soft object on the floor and roll around it as slowly as you can. Work closer and closer to the object, riding in tighter circles. Aim to get your rear wheel touching the object as you make super-tight turns. Now ride around it in the opposite direction.

SKILL 14: THE ENDO

Now that you have mastered all the skills that pivot from the rear axle, it's time to master pivoting over the front axle. The endo is mainly used by trials riders but that's not to say we should not become familiar with the feeling of pivoting over the front axle. Like the wheelie there is a neutral pivot point in the front centre where we can happily sit, balanced and poised. The skill can be very useful in tight, technical terrain as shown in the switchback, but you can also pivot around in a tight spot and ride back out. It is also immensely satisfying to perfect the nose wheelie.

Braking is a key thing here – the ability to blend the front brake in smoothly is vital. As with all skills, there are some safe ways to practise this technique. Find a safe spot with good visibility and a friendly surface.

- Roll along at walking pace in your neutral stance.

- Spot where you want to come to a stop.

- Feed the front brake in slowly while simultaneously popping up from your dipped heels.

- You need to lift the legs up into the torso to absorb the forward motion of the bike.

- This one really is down to speed control and feeling.

- Lower the bike back to the floor using the same technique in reverse.

Progress the technique

■ Place a marker on the floor. I use an empty plastic bottle as it will move easily and just collapse should I land on it.

■ Roll in at jogging pace in your neutral stance, focusing on the bottle.

■ As you approach spring up from your heels while simultaneously applying the front brake.

■ Try to make a turn around the marker in a nice, smooth radius.

■ Approach at different angles and ride imaginary lines around the bottle.

■ As you gain confidence try working on steeper gradients. Performing nose manuals down steeper banks will help build your confidence in avoiding those cold shower moments when thrown into a tight switchback on the trail. Experiment with wheel placement by planting the rear wheel onto a marked spot, curb, drink bottle etc.

■ Try doing an endo with your non-favoured foot leading.

■ Try going around the bottle in the opposite direction.

■ Try going around the bottle in the opposite direction with your non-favoured foot leading.

NOW GO RIDE YOUR BIKE AND HAVE FUN.

GLOSSARY

Ahead-set   Threadless steerer tube headset.

AM   Abbreviation for 'all-mountain'.

Anodising   A process that hardens the surface of aluminium using electrolysis.

ATB   All terrain bicycle.

Ball-burnished   A finish given to aluminium that toughens the surface.

Ballooner   Old post-war cycle.

Beater   Another name for a klunker.

Berms/bermed corner   Banked corners on a trail.

Billet   A solid piece of metal.

Blow through   When a bike uses all its suspension travel, it 'blows through' it.

BMB   British Mountain Bike Federation.

BMX   Bicycle motocross – standard bikes have small compact frames and use 20-inch wheels.

Bolt-through   System for holding a wheel hub in the frame or fork – an oversized, custom-made axle.

Bomber   Bike mass-produced by Raleigh in the early eighties and another name for a klunker.

Bottom bracket   The tube and junction located where the crank spindle bolts in.

Bottom out   To hit the bump stop on your suspension unit.

Braze-on   Additional mounting points that are welded to a frame including cable guides and pannier rack mounts.

Breezer   Nickname for Joe Breeze's first production bike.

Bunny hop   A skill where you lift the bike into the air whilst riding it.

Buzz   Noise created by high-frequency bumps.

Cadence braking   A method of braking that involves increasing and decreasing the amount of force you apply to the brake lever.

Cam   A reciprocating movement in relation to the knee joint and the pedal stroke.

Cassette   The cluster of cogs that bolt onto the free-hub body on the rear hub.

Chainring   Front drive ring connected to the crank arm via a spider, a section on the drive side crank arm.

Chain stay   The lower tube from the bottom bracket to the rear axle/dropout.

Chris King   American exotic component manufacturer.

CNC   Computer numerical control – a system used by computer-controlled mills and lathes to shape the billet, plate and bar.

Coasting   Rolling along without pedalling.

Cold shower Refers to the feeling of tensing up that you get if you jump into a cold shower.

Comp Abbreviation for 'competition'.

Compression The force exerted on you and your suspension.

Cranks The arms that the pedals and chainring connect to.

Cruiser Another name for a klunker.

Cup and cone The shape of opposing bearing surfaces.

Curb Concrete or stone pitching next to a tarmaced or paved road.

Derailleur The rear mechanism that the chain runs through, enabling you to change gear.

DH Abbreviation for 'downhill'.

DJ Abbreviation for 'dirt jump'.

Dirt jump A man-made feature to jump your bike from.

Downhill A point-to-point downhill time trial.

Drive train The drive system, chain, cranks, derailleurs and rear cassette.

Drop-off A trail feature that is too steep to ride down, you drop off it.

Dual slalom A downhill elimination race through marked gates, where two riders run head to head, in parallel lanes.

Elastomer Polymer used in suspension units.

Endo A skill where you put the bike up onto the front wheel.

Enduro Endurance racing.

ESE Entry/section/exit

4X Abbreviation for 'four cross', a discipline where four riders race head to head down a purpose built course.

FR Abbreviation for 'free-ride'.

Frame set The frame and fork.

Free-hub The part of the hub that gives forward motion and allows you to freewheel without the cranks moving.

Free-ride Where riders create lines in nature, often involving some large drops.

Front fork The part of a frame set that holds the front wheel.

Full suss Slang for 'full-suspension'.

Hard-tail Another name for a standard rigid mountain bike.

Head angle The angle at which the head tube sits in relation to a vertical plumb line.

Headset The component parts that allow the fork to fit and turn in the head tube.

Head tube The short front section of tube on a frame that houses the headset and fork steerer tube.

Heat treating A finishing process that frames go through to remove any impurities in the metal and stiffen the final finish.

High frequency Fast, close movement of the trail.

Hoops Another name for wheel rims or the wheel set.

Horst link The suspension linkage system created by Horst Leitne.

Hucking Dropping large features, typically associated with a manoeuvre that is not smooth.

IMBA International Mountain Bike Association.

Indexed Marked points where a gear is selected on a thumb shifter.

Klunker Name given to the old post-war newspaper-boy bike.

Klunkerz Another name for the group of riders that rode off-road in the Marin County area.

Lip The edge or launch point from a jump or drop.

Looping out Falling off the back of the bike.

Manual Roll along with the front wheel in the air.

Moped Motorised pedal scooter.

MTB Abbreviation for 'mountain bike'.

Neutral stance (or position) The standing riding position while coasting.

NORBA National Off-Road Bicycle Association.

Onza American component manufacturers.

Parkour A style of urban sport, also known as free-running.

Pre-load The amount of travel a suspension unit takes up when the rider's mass is added to the vehicle.

Presta valve Pointed valve, a narrower valve allowing rim manufacturers to produce stronger rims.

Psychosis A marathon downhill race that used to be run in British Columbia.

Pumping To move your body to gain extra momentum from the trail.

Q-factor The offset of your crank arms.

QR Abbreviation for 'quick-release'.

Rake The amount the fork leads in front – the distance between a virtual straight line drawn down the steerer tube and the front hub axle.

R&D Research and development.

Rear dropout Part of the frame where the rear wheel and derailleur locate.

Rebound The force that returns your suspension unit to its nominal position.

Repack A trail and timed downhill event in the Mount Tam area of San Francisco.

Rim Wheel rim.

Ringle American component manufacturer.

Rock Shox American suspension manufacturer.

Rohloff German manufacturer famous for high-quality internal gear hubs.

RPM Revolutions per minute.

RRE Roots/rocks/earth, also known as 'white noise'.

Sag/Droop The amount of pre-load you have on your suspension unit.

Schrader The standard car-type valve often found on suspension units, some manufacturers produce inner tubes with this valve type.

Seat stay The tube that runs from the top tube and seat tube junction down to the rear dropout, where the rear wheel and derailleur attach to the frame, where it meets the chain stay.

Seat tube The section of tube that your seat post slots into.

7stanes Seven trails in the Scottish Borders – a 'stane' is a stone. Each trail is made from the local stone, hence the name.

Shimano Component manufacturer founded in 1921 by Shozaburo Shimano, which began by producing freewheels.

Shock Abbreviation for 'shock absorber'.

Shore Abbreviation for 'north shore' – raised wooden trails/platforms of varying widths.

Single-ply Refers to the amount of thread in a tyre side wall – a single layer or weave.

Soft-tail Another name for a full-suspension bike.

SPD Shimano Pedal Dynamics – a design of clipless bicycle pedals.

SRAM Corporation Large American bicycle component manufacturer – the acronym comprises the names of the company founders Scott, Ray, Sam.

Steerer tube The section of tube on your front forks that inserts into the head tube and head set.

Switchback A very tight radius turn where the trail switches back on itself.

Top tube The tube that runs between the head tube and seat tube – the length of this tube is the critical measurement to get right when buying a mountain bike.

Track stand A skill where you balance your bike on the spot.

Trials A discipline in which riders have to complete marked sections without putting a foot down.

Two-ply Refers to the amount of thread in a tyre sidewall – two layers, or weaves, create a stronger sidewall.

UCC Union Confédérale de Coordination, French-based race organizer.

UCI Union Cycliste Internationale – the world's governing body for cycling, based in Switzerland.

U brakes U-shaped, cable-operated calliper brake.

Uphill A point-to-point uphill time trial.

Up-step A trail feature that you have to ride up onto, typically a boulder.

Visual cues/trail input Trail features, including RRE, to respond to or to perform on/off.

Wash out To slide out, lose control.

Wheelie A skill where you ride along with your front wheel in the air.

White noise The excess information around us that we need not pay attention to.

Work hardening A process that happens to aluminium when the metal is subjected to load and torsion, weakening its structure.

XC Abbreviation for 'cross country'.

Yule The motion of the vehicle beyond its neutral stance on its suspension components, tyres and shock absorbers.

FURTHER READING AND USEFUL WEBSITES

www.britishcycling.org.uk
Britain's governing body for cycling

www.scuonline.org
The cycling governing body for Scotland

www.uci.ch
The world governing body for cycling

www.imba.com
International mountain biking group liaising between landowners and mountain bikers.

www.ctc.org.uk
The UK's national cyclists' organisation

www.bikeradar.com
News and features on all aspects of biking

www.singletrackworld.com
Online cycling magazine, predominantly for cross country trail riders

Dirt.mpora.com
Cycling magazine for downhill riders

www.descent-world.co.uk
Online cycling magazine, predominantly for downhill riding

www.mtbskills.eu
The author's mountain bike training academy

INDEX

A

axles 30

B

bars 31, 112, 115–16
bikes 3–4, 11–31, 89–98
body armour 102–4
brakes 12–13, 21–2, 98, 112,
    114, 116–17
braking 130–5
bunny hops 87, 175–80

C

chainrings 14, 17, 26
clothing 13, 45, 101–2
clubs 7, 40–1
competitions 5–6, 7, 8–9, 25–6,
    55–87
core techniques *see* braking;
    cornering; looking; manuals;
    neutral stance; pumping;
    shifting gear
cornering 151–64
cranks 28, 113, 120
cross-country 58–62, 90–1

D

development of bikes 11–31
dirt jumping 23, 41–2, 93
downhill 42, 66–9, 72–7, 95–6,
    99
drive systems 114
drop offs 180–4
dual slalom 69–71

E

endo 193–5
endurance racing 77–8
enduro 84–6
equipment 45, 89–107
exercises 46–53, 56–7
eye wear 100

F

forks 19, 23, 122–5
four cross (4X) 71–2, 93
frames 6, 7, 18, 23–4, 30, 91,
    96–7
free-ride 26, 79–82, 87, 95, 99

G

gear sets 6, 26, 28, 98, 114
geometry 11, 97–8
gloves 100
grading system for trails 39
guides 38–9

H

headsets 28, 113
helmets 45, 99–100
history of mountain biking 3–9
hydration 44, 45, 104

I

inspection of bikes 111–15

J

jumps 184–8

K

kitsch events 87

L

long-travel bikes 95–6
looking 149–51

M

manuals 173–4
map reading 37
marathon downhill 72–7
medium-travel bikes 94

N

neutral stance 136–49
night-riding 41

P

pedals 13, 16, 113, 120, 166, 173
preparation for riding 44–5, 56–7
pumping 171–2

S

saddles 112, 118–19
set-up 57, 115–20, 127
Seven Deadly Spins project 37
shifting gear 139–40
shoes 100–1
short-travel bikes 92
slope style 79–82
spares:
    4X 72
    cross-country 62
    downhill 69
    dual slalom 71
    enduro 86
    marathon downhill 77
    slope style/free-ride 82
    street racing 83
    trials 66
    uphill 63
stems 116
street racing 23, 82–4, 93
suspension 18–19, 26, 120–9
switchbacks 188–93

T

trail centres 34–6
training:
    4X 72
    cross-country 59–60
    downhill 68
    dual slalom 70
    endurance racing 78
    enduro 86
    marathon downhill 75
    slope style/free-ride 80–1
    street racing 83
    trials 65
    uphill 63
trials 64–6, 94
tyres 11, 22, 105–7, 113, 121

U

Union Cycliste Internationale (UCI) 8–9, 58, 65, 74, 84
uphill 62–3
urban riding 43

W

wheel sets 20–1, 27, 30, 98
wheelies 166–70